Berlitz®

KU-013-006

VENICE

- A ✔ in the text denotes a highly recommended sight
- A complete A–Z of practical information starts on p.115
- Extensive mapping throughout: on cover flaps and in text

Printed in Switzerland by Weber SA, Bienne.

1st edition
November 1997

Although we make every effort to ensure the accuracy of the information in this guide, changes do occur. If you have any new information, suggestions or corrections to contribute, we would like to hear from you. Please write to Berlitz Publishing at the above address.

Text: Paul Murphy
Editors: Brigitte Lee, Delphine Verroest
Photography: Jon Davison
Layout: Cristina Silva
Cartography: Visual Image (pp. 28, 65 and 115)
                 🌐 Falk-Verlag, Hamburg (on cover)

Thanks to: Cesare Battisti of the Azienda Promozione Turistica for his invaluable assistance in the preparation of this guide.

Cover photographs: *The Grand Canal and Santa Maria della Salute*;
                     back: *View from the Campanile over the
                     Palazzo Ducale* – © Berlitz

Photo on p.4:   *St Mark's Basin, with San Giorgio Maggiore in
                 the background.*

CONTENTS

Venice and the Venetians

Venice is, quite simply, a city apart – a tantalizing blend of East and West, neither totally European nor wholly Italian. Traces of Byzantium and more distant oriental influences are everywhere apparent. Nestling in its lagoon, the city has an unsurpassed beauty which, made melancholy by picturesque decay, gives it a Romantic ambience that has inspired artists and travellers throughout the centuries. In a world where cities and countries are losing their identity to the expediency of mass marketing, Venice has preserved its cultural integrity, eschewing corporate anonymity for the welcome of traditional hospitality.

Although the great city fairly reeks of history and bustles with contemporary commerce, it can often seem artificial, unreal even. Were those incredibly ornate palaces inhabited by living people? Can a city really function if its 'streets are filled with water'? Some critics have even accused the city of being too absorbed in its own past; indeed, with its ageing population of 75,000 now less than half what it was in the 1930s, Venice does at times feel like a ghost town. Walk through the deserted streets at night (this is one of the safest cities in Europe) and you'll experience both Venice's charm and its malaise.

Walking is the only way to see the real city and Venice, perhaps more than any other place, is a series of magical visual vignettes: dark, narrow passageways that end in a sunlit square with a medieval wellhead; ancient street signs and stone reliefs at first-floor level; elderly women looking down from the upper floors of their crumbling houses, hauling up baskets of fruit and vegetables from street level; peeling shuttered windows belonging to a once glorious palace now falling into decay; a tiny stone bridge with a sleek black gondola moored beside. Remember, as you walk along, that the Venetian atmosphere is quite **5** unlike that of other, more ordinary cities. With so many narrow alleyways and bridges, a certain etiquette has to be observed – shoving and jostling are definitely discouraged and, of course, there is no escaping into the cocooned comfort of a motor vehicle.

When the walking gets tiring, take to the water aboard a *vaporetto* (waterbus), probably the most civilized and invigorating form of urban transport. As the breeze off the water ruffles your hair, watch exquisite medieval *palazzi* peer over their own reflections before sliding by, leaving you to contemplate the distant memory of bottlenecks and exhaust fumes.

This supremely improbable city rests on an archipelago of 118 flat islets, whose buildings are supported by countless millions of larch poles driven into the sediment. It is comprised of six *sestieri* (districts), and subdivided into a further 33 *parrochie* (parishes), each a small village with its own distinctive flavour. Criss-crossing Venice is a labyrinth of 177 canals spanned by some 450 bridges.

The canals are partly flushed out by the tides that sweep in daily from the Adriatic through three seaways which pierce the ring of sand bars (*lidi*) protecting the lagoon.

The sea, from which Venice draws its energy, has always been linked inextricably with the city's fortunes. The modern substitute for the riches once brought back to Venice by merchant and warrior fleets alike is tourism, to which the city devotes much of its considerable energy. Nowhere else has the practice of relieving visitors of their currency become such a refined art. But what delights you get in return!

Visitors will find Venetians friendly, immensely fond of children, professedly romantic, very hospitable, proud of being well-dressed, frequently self-infatuated and possibly just a trifle patronizing towards anyone unlucky enough to have been born somewhere else.

Their somewhat obscure dialect emphasizes the separateness of Venice, and unless lost, visitors are often amused to see the names of canals or dis-

The romantic Grand Canal at dusk, as seen from the splendid vantage point of the Rialto Bridge.

tricts spelled differently from one sign to another.

Despite its manifold charms, Venice does have its share of detractors, who complain that the city is overpriced, that there are too many crowds and, perhaps worst of all, that the canals give off a rather unpleasant odour in summer. Do not be deterred. Such critics probably ventured no further than the Piazza (around half the city's visitors are day-trippers). This is certainly not to diminish the importance of the world's most beautiful square, nor the fabulous Basilica and equally magnificent Doges' Palace. Even at the height of the season, however, you can see them without being jostled. Simply arrange to visit early or late in the day, when all the trippers have departed. You will be astonished at how quickly the crowds melt away within just a few hundred yards of the Piazza, at any time of the day, or season.

Of course Venice is expensive in and around the Piazza. But those famous cafés do display their prices quite prominently. Besides, the stunning location more than compensates for the financial expenditure. Step a few yards away from the Piazza, however, and a glass of wine and a snack with the locals will cost you no more (and quite often much less) than its London or Parisian equivalent. Remember that much of the produce consumed in Venice has to be brought in by small boats. The absence of large-scale transportation does make for a picturesque city, but at a cost.

Venetians are notably proud of their city and its glowing history, and are both frustrated and amused by the fact that many visitors' Venetian expe-

There's always hustle and bustle around the Doges' Palace, but off the beaten track, Venice may seem surprisingly sleepy.

8

rience begins and ends starring in a photograph with the pigeons of San Marco. The locals will try to encourage you off the beaten track, to see the treasures of the Dorsoduro and Castello districts, and the other *sestieri*. It is advice which all visitors should heed.

Perhaps we should leave the final word to another local, the 18th-century dramatist Carlo Goldoni, founder of Italian realistic comedy. He observed: 'Venice is a city that is so unreal, that one cannot have any idea of what she is like unless one has actually beheld her.'

A Brief History

It may be hard to believe today but this tiny city, now financially dependent on tourism, was once the centre of the most important and powerful state in all of Europe; as the 'Queen of the Seas' (*Serenissima*), it was renowned for its maritime prowess, rapacious trading ambitions and shrewd negotiating instincts. During this time, Venice indelibly influenced the course of modern history, and left us an incomparable legacy in the shape of the city itself.

Early Venetians

Fishermen and boatmen skilled at navigating the shallow lagoon's silt and sand islands were in fact the first Venetians, although the first major settlement came about as a result of the invasion of the Lombards in AD 568. This barbarian onslaught sent the coastal dwellers fleeing to the low-lying offshore islands in the lagoon, first to Torcello, then out to Malamocco on the string of *lidi*

exposed to the Adriatic. Refugees from the mainland had taken flight here before, during the previous century, escaping from Attila the Hun, but this time they decided to stay.

Venetia, or Venezia, was the name of the entire area at the northern end of the Adriatic under the Roman empire. The beginning of the Venice that we know today developed very gradually around a cluster of small islands, including that of Rivo Alto, the future Rialto. The lagoon islands remained free of the Lombard kingdom that held much of northern Italy in sway and were only subject to loose control from the Roman-Byzantine centre at Ravenna (which was itself subject to Constantinople).

Some time around the turn of the 8th century (either 697 or 726) the lagoon communities were united under a separate military command, set up at Malamocco under a *dux* (Latin for leader) or doge. Though the first doges were probably selected by the lagoon dwellers, they still took orders from the Byzantine emperor.

HISTORICAL LANDMARKS

568	Mainland communities flee to the islands.
697 or 726	Island communities unite, first doge elected.
810	Venice resists attack by Charlemagne's son.
c. 829	Body of St Mark stolen and brought to Venice.
1000	Dalmatian rivals defeated in battle for Adriatic.
1104	Arsenal shipyards founded.
1199-1204	Fourth crusade; sack of Constantinople.
1253	First War with Genoa.
1297	Great Council established.
1310	Tiepolo's Revolt crushed, Council of Ten formed.
1380	Genoa finally defeated in the Fourth Genoese War.
1453	Loss of Constantinople to the Ottomans.
1508-10	League of Cambrai inflicts losses on Venice, but self-destructs.
1571	Ottomans defeated at the battle of Lepanto.
1669	Fall of Crete to the Turks.
1718	Venice loses the Peloponnese, its last real territory in the eastern Mediterranean.
1797	Napoleon abolishes the Republic, then trades it to Austro-Hungary.
1805	Napoleon wins back Venice.
1815	Napoleon defeated in 1814, Venice returns to Austro-Hungary in 1815.
1848-9	Venetian patriot, Daniele Manin (see p.16), leads an uprising.
1866	Austro-Hungary defeated by Prussia. Venice joins the new Italy.
1928	Porto Marghera completed.
1966	Worst lagoon flooding of modern times instigates Venice in Peril Fund (see p.32).

The Lombards were succeeded on the mainland in 774 by king Charlemagne's Frankish army and in 810 his son Pépin was sent to conquer the offshore upstart. Pépin seized Malamocco but the doge and his entourage managed to escape to the safety of Rivo Alto, where they settled the new seat of the fledgling republic and built a fortress on the site now occupied by the Doges' Palace.

The Rise of the Republic

The new city gradually became independent of distant Byzantium and prospered, first from its tight control of the north Italian river deltas and subsequently from the sea itself.

Fishing, salt and the lumber trade, together with the transport of slaves, enriched the city and any rival producer or trader was soon ruthlessly put out of business.

From the 9th century, Venice dared to traffic with the Moslems in defiance of both pope and Byzantine emperor. With Moslem gold and silver,

the Venetians brought exotic Eastern luxuries from Constantinople and traded them at a high profit with the rest of Europe. By this time, Venice was no longer dependent on the Eastern Empire and, sometime around 829, demonstrated as much by snatching the body of St Mark the Evangelist to replace the Byzantine saint, Theodore, as their patron.

As soon as the precious relic reached Venice, construction of a chapel was begun next to the Doges' Palace: the original basilica of San Marco. Venice quickly adopted the evangelist and the accompanying winged lion as the city's symbol.

The newly founded Arsenal turned out fleets of stronger and swifter galleys, enabling Venice to move deeper down into the Adriatic where it warred for decades with its bitter enemies, the powerful but less organized Dalmatian fleet. In the

*V*enice's ethereal light has enchanted and inspired artists over the centuries.

13

year 1000, the republic scored a significant victory against the Dalmatians, which it celebrated with a 'wedding of the sea' ceremony which can still be seen to this day (see p.103). Ships flying St Mark's pennant ranged over the Aegean Sea and the eastern Mediterranean, trading and plundering, then faithfully bringing back spoils to enrich the doges' treasury and further strengthen the state. Venice soon came to be known as the *Serenissima*, or 'Queen of the Seas'.

Empire-Building

From the start of the Crusades in 1095, the Venetians sensed rich pickings. Well positioned, politically and geographically, between Europe and the East, and with little concern for the spiritual aspects of the campaigns, they eagerly produced and outfitted ships, equipped knights and often charged extortionate prices for the voyage to the holy places. Sometimes, these religious warriors were used to settle Venice's commercial quarrels along the way,

much to the pope's disapproval. In the course of the 12th century, the Venetians were just as successful at piracy as the Genoese, Greeks, Saracens, Pisans and Sicilians marauding around the Mediterranean.

A proud diplomatic moment came in 1177, when Venice supervised the peace process between the Holy Roman Emperor, Frederick I (known as Barbarossa), and Pope Alexander III. Much less proud was Venice's ruthless leading role in the Fourth Crusade of 1199-1204, which culminated in the sack of Constantinople.

Once again, Venetian equipment and transport were hired, but when the assembled Crusaders came to meet in Venice, they were short of their expected numbers and found themselves unable to pay the agreed amount. Some versions of history maintain that Venice actually schemed its way into this position by negotiating a fixed fee in advance and then leaking propaganda to deter Crusaders. Whatever the truth, a deal was made that the Crusaders would temporarily join arms with the Venetian army, and the journey to the Holy Land was diverted to Constantinople. This sacred capital of Christian civilization since the 4th century was once Venice's overlord, but now it became its slave as the city was brutally pillaged with terrible loss of life. One-quarter of the booty was given to a new emperor installed by Doge Enrico Dandolo's forces; the remainder was divided up between the Venetians and the hapless Crusaders, who had to hand over most of their share to their allies to cover their debts.

Venice also began modestly calling itself 'Lord and Master of a Quarter and a Half-Quarter of the Empire of Romania', or eastern Roman empire. The republic was now clearly a world power, controlling all the major points along the routes to Egypt and the Crimea. The brutal saga of Constantinople, however, made its name despised throughout much of the civilized world.

At the end of the 13th century, the Venetians curbed the power of the doges by converting from a monarchy to a patrician oligarchy. The ruling Great Council was enlarged to over 1,000 noble members and the aristocracy settled in power by means of a Council of Ten (responsible for state security) and other commissions.

Marco Polo

Venice's most famous citizen opened the eyes of 13th-century Europe to the irresistibly exotic mysteries of the Orient. For some 20 years, Marco Polo served the Mongol Emperor Kublai Khan. He was the first Westerner permitted to travel about freely in China.

Polo's voyages opened up new routes for the spice trade. When he came back from China, legend has it that no one recognized him or believed his tales – until the returning hero slit the seams of his clothes and precious jewels fell out.

15

Eventually, doges became little more than pampered prisoners in their magnificent palace, stripped of every vestige of authority and forbidden to contact the outside world without their counsellors' consent. From their election, by a complicated procedure, until their death, their primary function was to preside over the republic's pompous festivities. After 1310, no major change was made in the constitution until the republic fell in 1797.

Wars and Intrigue

Venice spent much of the 14th century battling with her deadly rival, Genoa. The two great maritime powers fought most bitterly over the slave and grain trade in the Black Sea and the route out of the Mediterranean and north to Bruges or Antwerp. There, spices and other Oriental wares could be traded for prized Flemish cloth, English wool and tin. Both states also transported salt from the Balearic island of Ibiza and sweet Greek wines through the Straits of Gibraltar.

In 1379, during the fourth and final Genoese War, Venice came closer to defeat than at any time in its history. The Genoese fleet, aided by Hungarian and Paduan troops, captured and sank Venetian ships in home waters; raiding parties, meanwhile, burned settlements along the Lido and closed off all mainland escape routes. When the key port of Chioggia, just south of Venice, was stormed and taken, the *Serenissima* seemed lost.

The beleaguered city rallied, blockading the Lido lagoon entrance with ships chained together and audaciously closing the door behind its attackers by sinking barges laden with rocks in the channels to Chioggia. Mounting cannons on galleys for the first time, and hiring the best available mercenaries, the Venetians retook the port and in 1380 Genoa surrendered, finished for ever as a major maritime force.

The 14th century also saw domestic difficulties. In 1310 a group of disgruntled aristocrats under Baiamonte Tiepolo tried to seize power and kill

The Old Lady of the Mortar

Step off the Piazza through the archway of the famous Torre dell'Orologio and, a few yards along on the left, look upwards for a stone relief of an old woman. This relief commemorates one of the city's favourite legends.

On the night of 15 June 1310, an old woman looked out of her window to find out what all the commotion was below. She saw the revolutionary army of Baiamonte Tiepolo heading into the Piazza to do battle with the doge. By accident (or design), she knocked (or threw) a stone mortar off her window sill on to the head of Tiepolo's flag bearer, felling him and sending the rebels back to the Rialto in confusion. The threat was over and the old lady became a heroine of the republic.

the doge, but their revolt was quickly crushed. Much worse was to come. Between 1347 and 1349, almost half of the city's population of 120,000 was wiped out by the Black Death. A further 20,000 Venetians died in another epidemic in 1382, and over the next three centuries, the city was almost never free of plague. At the Rialto, a major European commercial banking centre, fortunes were made and lost as the republic bartered, badgered and borrowed to support its costly wars with Genoa.

Recovery after the Genoese wars came quickly, however, and the republic then began to focus attention on its landside boundary. As an expanding manufacturing city in the 15th century, it needed food, wood and metal from the nearest possible sources. However, its push along the northern Italian rivers and across the plain of Lombardy soon met with opposition, and conflicts kwnown as the Lombard wars began in 1425. The republic defended its new territory so tenaciously that both Milan, Florence and Naples formed an anti-Venice coalition. Europe worried that Venice might take over the entire Italian peninsula.

17

New Threats

However, a new and menacing rival arose in the East against Venice: the Ottoman Empire. The new young sultan, Mohammed the Conqueror, was not taken seriously and the forces sent to protect Constantinople proved inadequate. In 1453, the city fell into Turkish hands. In the following years, the Turks harassed Venetian trade routes and won a key naval battle at Negroponte in the north Aegean in 1470. Although the *Serenissima* was still the leading Mediterranean maritime power, these defeats marked the beginning of a long downhill slide.

While its fortunes beyond the lagoon waned, Venice became the centre of a magnificent cultural outpouring. There was no more sumptuous building in the Western world than the Doges' Palace, no church filled with as many exotic treasures as San Marco. Artists like the Bellinis, Giorgione, Carpaccio, Tintoretto, Veronese and Titian flourished; Andrea Palladio's revolutionary concepts shaped the future of modern architecture; the republic's lawyers, physicians, mathematicians, printers and Greek scholars were famed throughout the West. Venice was now the richest city in all Europe.

Other threats were looming; the world was changing, quite literally. In 1498, Vasco da Gama of Portugal undertook his epic voyage around the Cape of Good Hope to India, thus opening up new and more direct trade routes and putting an end to Venice's spice-trade monopoly. During the same period of prodigious exploration, Christopher Columbus's landfalls on the other side of the Atlantic also proved momentous for the Venetian republic: Europe gradually turned towards the Western hemisphere, losing interest in the oriental trade which had ensured Venetian prosperity for so long.

Decline and Decadence

Following the French invasion of Italy in 1494, Venice sought to capture territories closer to home and, using its renowned

18

international skills, successfully played off the various warring parties to its advantage, further encroaching on Italy.

However, this international brinkmanship so incensed the rest of Europe that, under the auspices of Pope Julius II and the King of Spain, a pan-European organization known as the League of Cambrai was formed in 1508, with the intention of destroying the republic.

First, the pope excommunicated Venice. Like many other Vatican decrees though, this one was largely ignored. Next, city after city defected as the republic's 20,000-man mercenary army fell apart. For a while, things seemed desperate, but the League fell apart in internecine struggles and Venice managed to regain nearly all its territories. The seven-year war had cost the Venetian coffers dearly, and the *Serenissima*'s ambitions in Italy were well and truly quashed. Furthermore, with Charles V's empire steadily accumulating Italian territory, all of Venice's diplomatic skill was needed to preserve its own independence.

Around the Mediterranean, the Ottomans surged on. From Albania all the way along to Morocco, the coast became Turkish. The naval battle which finally turned the Turkish tide was fought in 1571, at Lepanto in Greece, with the combined Christian fleet spearheaded by Venetian galleys. However, the allies, by now quite suspicious of Venice (and with good reason), made sure that the city did not profit from this. Instead of continuing the offensive east, they actually signed away

*T*he winged Lion of St Mark – proud symbol of the city ever since the 9th century.

19

the Venetian stronghold of Cyprus as part of the peace treaty.

At home, plague raged once again and, between 1575 and 1577, the populace dwindled from 150,000 to 100,000 in the last major outbreak of the plague. Paradoxically, in spite of epidemics, famine and a diminished empire, the city managed to prosper through the 16th and 17th centuries, aided by the skills and useful contacts of its Jewish refugees.

And, always, the pilgrims and tourists came. Unlike many other European cities, Venice had never been occupied by a foreign army and its treasures remained intact. With Claudio Monteverdi in the 17th century and Antonio Vivaldi in the 18th, Venice produced more operas and had more opera houses than any other European city. Tiepolo and Canaletto painted Venice into the international consciousness. Carlo Goldoni's new adaptations of *commedia dell'arte* broke exciting theatrical ground, while Venetian girls' choirs, set designers, or-

ganists and organ builders were the toast of Europe.

If the city was a fading world power, it quickly warmed to its new role as the playground of Europe, staging wild carnival balls and becoming infamous for its comely courtesans and extravagant gambling. Those two famous coffee houses which still grace Piazza San Marco opened in the 18th century, becoming the fashionable meeting spots for the idle rich of Venice and the grandest of 'Grand Tourists'. Hardly any-

body noticed the republic's last naval adventures – skirmishes with Barbary pirates off the North African coast.

This period may be seen as the final throes of the republic. Everyone knew Napoleon was coming, but by now the city was too weak to stop him.

The End of the Republic

Napoleon Bonaparte entered the city, thundering that he would be the new 'Attila' of the lagoon. He demanded that the government turn its power over to a democratic council under French military protection, and in 1797 the last doge, Ludovico Manin, abdicated and the Great Council voted to dissolve itself. The *Serenissima* was no more.

The French troops looted the treasures and destroyed the Arsenal. Napoleon stayed in Venice only for five months,

*G*uardi's painting of the Bucintoro *underscores Venice's prime role as a maritime power.* **21**

relinquishing it to Austrian control. In 1805 he was back, having defeated the Austrians at Austerlitz, and made the city part of his short-lived Kingdom of Italy. After Waterloo, the Austrians again occupied Venice, and stayed for over 50 years until 1866.

The Austrians were despised by the citizenry, but at least they restored to the city most of the artistic booty taken by Napoleon. In 1846 they linked Venice to the mainland for the first time, erecting an unsightly railway bridge.

In 1848, the Venetians under Daniele Manin rose up and ousted the Austrian garrison. They declared an independent 'republic' which was to hang on for 17 hard months of bombardment, blockade and cholera before returning to the Austrian fold. Manin and the other leaders were exiled.

In 1866, after Austria's defeat by Prussia, the Venetians voted overwhelmingly in a referendum to join the new Kingdom of Italy and eventually became the capital of one of **22** the peninsula's 20 regions.

The Modern City

Virtually untouched by the two world wars, Venice has now become a comparative political backwater, but it has also undergone some dramatic and important changes.

In a post-war referendum, the Venetians and other Italians voted to abolish the monarchy and become a republic. Tourism boomed once more and manufacturing in the traditional industries revived. One major industrial development was the construction of the Porto Marghera complex on the mainland. It has, in fact, drawn Venice's young working population away from the old city to live in the faceless suburbs of Mestre. In 1936 the population of Venice was 170,000. Today it is less than 75,000.

Porto Marghera has caused significant pollution problems: blackening buildings, provok-

The view from the Campanile is Venice's finest; those exotic domes belong to the Basilica.

ing a harmful build-up of algae and, by tapping water from the lagoon, creating both flooding and sinking conditions. Since the (literal) watershed of flood waters in 1966, Venice and the international community have been stirred into action to save and revive the ancient fabric of the city. The Italian government erected huge mobile barriers in an attempt to control the tides through the lagoon and prevent further flooding.

Paradoxically, the biggest problem is also the city's most lucrative trade – tourism. At peak season, a daily influx of over 25,000 tourists takes its toll on the city's fragile infrastructure and threatens to destroy the very sights they have come to admire. Tighter control on the number of visitors, together with strict measures to counter the risk of flooding (see p.32), control pollution and reverse the decline in the young population, are all problems which must be addressed to enable the city to face the future with confidence.

What to See

Venice may initially appear a confusing maze of waterways and walkways, but after a day or two it's surprisingly easy to get your bearings in what turns out to be a compact, logically arranged city. A useful guide to orientation is to divide the Grand Canal into four roughly delineated portions: north-east (Cannaregio), north-west (San Polo and Santa Croce), south-east (San Marco and Castello) and south-west (Dorsoduro). The tourist office provides a free map of the city, but if you intend exploring the labyrinth of Venice's tiny alleyways in any detail, it is worthwhile investing in something a bit more comprehensive, such as Hallwag's 1:5,500 city map.

Popular meeting places are the countless piazzas, squares (*campi*) or waterfront promenades (*fondamente*). Watch out for old signs, usually placed quite high on the wall, which indicate the way (most commonly) to the Rialto, Piazzale Roma or Piazza San Marco and to specific tourist attractions as well as to *vaporetto* (waterbus) and *traghetto* (ferry) stages.

San Marco

One place that every visitor heads for in Venice is the Piazza San Marco; indeed, for at least half of all the city's visitors, Venice *is* the Piazza. *Vaporetti*, *motoscafi* (water taxis), private boats, warship launches and cruise liners all decant here, while from the other direction, tour groups snake their way through the colonnades of the square rallying relentlessly to their leader's upheld umbrella. However, before you make straight for the basilica or the Doges' Palace – or even Florian's for coffee – pause a while for an overview of the city.

CAMPANILE DI SAN MARCO

Where better to start your tour of Venice than at the top of St Mark's Bell Tower? For the most breathtaking view of the Piazza and arguably over all of

VENICE HIGHLIGHTS

(See also Museum and Gallery Highlights on p.41)
For those on a brief visit, or for your first day, here are Venice's principal highlights. The nearest *vaporetto* stop is indicated in brackets.

Accademia, Dorsoduro (*Accademia*); tel. 522 22 47. Five centuries of magnificent Venetian art. 9am-7pm daily (see pp.48-51).

Basilica di San Marco, Piazza di San Marco (*San Marco*). The spiritual heart of Venice, where East meets West. 9.45am-5pm Monday-Saturday, 2-5pm Sunday; Pala d'Oro and Treasury closed Sunday morning (see p.30).

Burano (*No. 12 vaporetto from Fondamente Nuove*). Picture-postcard fishing island of brightly coloured houses (see p.93).

Campanile di San Marco, Piazza di San Marco (*San Marco*); tel. 522 40 64. View of Venice from its highest point. 9.30am-4.30pm daily (Nov-Mar), 9.30am-7pm (Apr-Oct) (see p.24).

Collezione Guggenheim, Palazzo Venier dei Leoni, San Gregorio (*Accademia* or *Salute*); tel. 520 62 88. One of Europe's finest collections of modern art. 11am-6pm Wednesday-Monday (see p.51).

Grand Canal. Take the *No. 1 vaporetto* and admire the wonderful palaces on the world's most beautiful 'Main Street' (see p.63).

Rialto Markets. Venice's liveliest alleyways, full of fresh produce and local shoppers. 8am-noon Monday-Saturday (see p.58).

Scuola di San Giorgio degli Schiavoni, Ponte dei Greci, Castello (*Riva degli Schiavoni*); tel. 522 88 28. Masterpieces by Carpaccio in an intimate setting. 10am-12.30pm and 3-6pm Tuesday-Saturday, 10am-12.30pm Sunday (Nov-Mar); 9.30am-12.30pm and 3-6.30pm Tuesday-Saturday, 10am-12.30pm Sunday (Apr-Oct) (see p.46).

Scuola Grande di San Rocco, Campo San Rocco (*San Tomà*); tel. 523 48 64. Breathtaking large-scale works by Tintoretto in an opulent hall. 9am-5.30pm daily (Apr-Oct), 10am-1pm Monday-Friday and 10am-4pm Saturday-Sunday (Nov-Mar) (see p.60).

Torcello (*No. 12 vaporetto from Fondamente Nuove*). Tiny island offering pastoral tranquillity and a beautiful cathedral (see p.95). **25**

the city, simply step into the lift and ascend the 99m (324ft) of Venice's tallest building.

Within less than a minute, the exotic domes of the basilica, the splendid wedge-shaped tip of Dorsoduro (marking the end of the Grand Canal) and the island church of St Giorgio Maggiore lie beneath your feet, while all around you are the terracotta-coloured tiles of the ancient city roofscape.

The scene must look much the same now as it did over 200 years ago, when Goethe came here for his first view of the sea. It may well even look the same as four centuries ago when, according to local lore, Galileo brought the doge up here to show off his new telescope. Intriguingly, you cannot see a single canal from the Campanile – the perspective simply does not allow it.

This most potent symbol of the city, which in its time has served as lighthouse, gun turret and belfry, is not the original tower; that one crumpled into the Piazza on 14 July 1902. Fortunately, it had creaked and groaned so much in advance

that everyone knew what was coming and kept well away; the eventual collapse caused very little damage. Contrary to the 'evidence' of cleverly faked postcards on sale throughout the city, the moment was never caught on film.

The city council quickly decided to rebuild the bell tower 'as it was, where it was'. Exactly one thousand years after the erection of the original Campanile, on 25 April 1912, the new, lighter version was inaugurated, delighting Venice-lovers around the world, many of whom had contributed funds for the project.

PIAZZA SAN MARCO

With somewhat uncharacteristic modesty, Venetians call St Mark's Square simply the *Piazza*, since it is the only square in the city deemed worthy of the name. Napoleon was more fulsome; he reputedly called it the 'drawing room of Europe', a phrase repeated countless times each day by tour group leaders. Indeed, despite the throngs, it remains a supremely civilized place. What other square in the world is so elegantly proportioned (with colonnades on three sides), fringed with such exquisite monuments, or echoes to the sound of classical orchestras and is completely free of traffic?

The Piazza is actually a trapezoid, its uneven pavement sloping slightly downwards towards the basilica. The trachyte (volcanic rock) paving strips, more than 250 years old, lie over five or six earlier layers of tiles dating back to the mid-13th century. Indeed, the square was originally the site of a monastery garden with a canal running through it, but since its transformation in the 12th-13th centuries it has become the religious and political centre of the city. Splendid processions – at their height

There's been a Campanile in the Piazza for over a thousand years, but today's monolith is less than 90 years old.

27

| | 0 | 250 metre |
| | 0 | 250 yards |

Torre dell' Orologio

Procuratie Vecchie

Salizzada San Provolo

San Zaccaria

Campo San Zaccaria

Rio dei Vin

Piazza San Marco

Basilica di San Marco

Ponte dei Sospiri (Bridge of Sighs)

Procuratie Nuove

Tourist Information

Libreria Vecchia

Riva degli Schiavoni

Palazzo Ducale

Ponte dei Paglia

San Zaccaria

Riva degli Schiavoni 6,10,14,15,20

Giardini ex Reali (Royal Gardens)

Libreria Sansoviniana

San Marco Giardinetti

1

5

5,8

1,2,4

Canale di San Marco

2

4

3

probably unrivalled anywhere in the world – were staged here; one is brilliantly illustrated in Gentile Bellini's famous painting at the Accademia (see p.48). Most of the buildings around the square are 400-500 years old, and can be readily identified in many Venetian Renaissance paintings.

The Piazza has always attracted large crowds. Victorious commanders returning home from the Genoese or Turkish wars were fêted in front of the basilica with grand parades, while vendors sold sweets and snacks much as they do today. In the arcades, merchants transacted business while European knights and clergymen bought souvenirs and provisions for their crusades and pilgrimages to the Holy Land.

Here is a brief tour round the Piazza in an anti-clockwise direction, starting from the left of St Mark's Basilica.

The small square next to the basilica is known as the **Piazzetta del Leoncini**, after the two small marble lions which have been here ever since 1722. Aside from feeding the ubiquitous pigeons in the Piazza, another children's favourite is to come and straddle these glorious tame beasts.

The Campanile, however, is not the Piazza's only notable bell tower. The graceful **Torre dell'Orologio** (Clock Tower) has been telling the time for almost 500 years. Over the centuries, the two famous Moors atop the clock tower have been hammering the hours on their great bell, but have still put only a slight dent in it.

Normally it is possible to get to the top alongside them, and the sound of their hammer blows can be quite a shock to the ears. Venetians even claim that a workman in the 19th century was knocked clean off the top of the tower by one of the Moors' hammers. It is tempting to think that this was some kind of Revenge of the Moors, tired of enduring the impertinence of thousands of visitors wanting to test the old Venetian legend which confers sexual potency for the following year on anyone stroking the Moors' exposed nether regions.

For the foreseeable future, the Moors are safe, however, as the tower is closed to the public as part of a long-term restoration plan.

The Torre dell'Orologio features one of Venice's most colourful Lions of St Mark and a splendid **zodiacal clock** which shows the time in Arabic and Roman numerals. On epiphany in January and all through Ascension week in May, three bright-eyed Magi and a trumpeting angel swing out of the face of the clock tower on the stroke of every hour and, stiffly bowing, rotate around a gilded madonna.

Atop the Torre dell'Orologio, the Moors have been striking the time since the days of Columbus.

29

The colonnaded range adjacent to the Clock Tower was built around the same period, as home to the Procurators of San Marco, those state officers charged with the administration of the *sestieri*. It is known as the **Procuratie Vecchie** and serves as offices today. Below it are various shops and one of Venice's two most famous **cafés**, the Caffè Quadri, favoured haunt of the Austrians during their occupation in the 19th-century .

At the end of the Piazza opposite the basilica, there once stood the Church of San Gemniamo; but in 1807 Napoleon ordered it to be demolished to make way for a wing joining the two sides of the square, the *Ala Napoleonica* ('Napoleon's Wing'). On the front of the wing are several statues of Roman emperors and a central niche, originally intended for a statue of the Little Emperor himself, but which was pointedly left empty.

Opposite the Procuratie Vecchie is the **Procuratie Nuove**, built between 1582 and 1640 as a new home for the Procura-tors, and later occupied by Napoleon as a royal palace. The Museo Correr (see p.40) now occupies most of the upper floors of the *Ala Napoleonica* and this wing.

Below the Procuratie Nuove is the Piazza's other famous café, Florian's. It claims to be the oldest in the world, established in 1720, and has a charming, romantic mid-19th century interior.

BASILICA DI SAN MARCO

Combining an intriguing blend of mysterious eastern and glorious western elements, Venice's St Mark's Basilica is a truly magnificent shrine, encapsulating the old republic's grandiose view of itself as the worthy successor to Constantinople. Despite the sloping irregular floors, an eclectic mix

*T*he magnificent mosaics on the front of the Basilica di San Marco are a foretaste of the opulence within.

of styles both inside and out, five low domes of totally unequal proportions and some 500 non-matching columns, San Marco still manages to convey an immense sense of harmonious beauty.

The church was first built in 830 as a chapel for the doges and also to house the mortal remains of St Mark, recently stolen from Alexandria by two Venetian adventurers (see p.13). According to legend, they hid the body in a consignment of pork in order to deter the Moslems from searching them. Not only were the body and many of the adornments in the basilica stolen from the East; most of the church's columns are in fact prizes of conquest, brought back as booty from forays into the Levant.

The basilica became the republic's shrine and was the coronation and burial place of its doges. In 976, the original, largely wooden, church burned down and the basilica we see today was constructed between 1063 and 1094.

The narthex (the small porch at the entrance to the cathedral) is a good place to begin your acquaintance with the magical **mosaics** which are a predominant feature of the church interior. (In total, they are said to cover around 0.5ha, or 1 acre.) The mosaics in the narthex are some of the most beautiful of all, dating from the 13th century, and depict Old Testament events (Noah and the Flood is a favourite theme).

Take the staircase immediately to the right of the main entrance; this will lead you to a small museum where the prize exhibits are a splendid wooden Lion of St Mark and the cover for the Pala d'Oro (see p.34). However, the best reason for coming up here is to see the famous **horses of San Marco**. Cast in Rome, or possibly Greece, in around AD 200, they are the world's only surviving ancient *quadriga* (group of four horses abreast).

At one time, the *quadriga* crowned Trajan's Arch in Rome; then it was moved to the imperial hippodrome in Constantinople, where Doge Dan-

Venice in Peril

Following the disastrous floods of 1966, local and international funds under the collective title of 'Venice in Peril' were set up to restore buildings and works of art in the city, thus bringing Venice's plight to world attention. At that time the city was actually sinking, a problem caused by the industrial complex of Porto Marghera drawing off millions of gallons of lagoon water. That particular problem has subsequently been rectified, but massive pollution-related problems do still remain and the increasing regularity of the city's winter 'aqua alta' (high-water flooding) is a symptom of this.

Various long-term plans and projects have been formulated to protect Venice, but to date these have all been frustrated by a combination of factors, not least of which is the notorious Italian bureaucratic system.

The much travelled, priceless Horses of San Marco are glittering trophies of war.

dolo claimed it as spoils of war in 1204 and brought it back to Venice. After guarding the Arsenal shipyard for a while, the horses were moved to the front of the cathedral and became almost as symbolic of the city as its famous lion.

In 1378 the rival republic of Genoa boasted that it would 'bridle those unbridled horses' – but it never did. Napoleon did corral them, however, and had them taken to Paris to stand (appropriately enough) on the Place du Carrousel for some 13 years. The Austrians then restored them to San Marco and there they remained until World War I, when the Italian government moved them to Rome. During World War II the horses were again moved, this time into the nearby countryside. They will – the Venetians vow – never be allowed to leave again. The *quadriga* has been

forced, however, to make one more short move. The horses that now stand outside on the front of the basilica are replica; the originals have in fact been brought inside to protect them against the corrosive effect of atmospheric pollution.

From the museum, you have an excellent view of the galleried walkways all around the upper level of the cathedral (unfortunately they are never open to the public). However, you can enjoy spectacular elevated views from outside by stepping onto the balcony, with its pigeon's-eye view over the Piazza and Piazzetta.

Back down inside the basilica, take a look at the Treasury, **33** off the baptistery on the basilica's right side. Here are displayed yet more riches, looted from Constantinople at the time of the 4th Crusade of 1204. Next, turn your attention to the high altar, which bears a *ciborium* (canopy) mounted on four alabaster columns, dating from the 7th or 8th century, on which are sculpted scenes from the lives of Christ and the Virgin Mary. In the illuminated grating is a sarcophagus containing the relics of St Mark.

Behind the altar is one of Christendom's greatest treasures. The **Pala d'Oro** (golden altar screen) was crafted in the 10th century in Constantinople and embellished and enlarged several times on doges' orders until it reached its present stage in the mid-14th century. The screen contains dozens of biblical scenes and is constantly surrounded by hordes of sightseers, drawn by its sheer opulence. The exquisitely wrought golden frame holds Venice's equivalent of the Crown Jewels: 1,300 pearls, 400 garnets, 300 sapphires, 300 emeralds, 90 amethysts, 75 balas-rubies, some 15 rubies, four topazes and two cameos.

On a practical note: although all Venice's churches have a dress code, the basilica actually employs a doorperson to enforce it. Knee-length shorts are permissible, but short shorts are definitely not, while shoulders and backs must be covered. The basilica is generally dark and brooding, but is illuminated daily from 11.30am until 12.30pm and on Saturday and Sunday afternoon, making

One of the most pleasant pastimes in Venice is simply to watch the world glide by.

this is a good time to see the mosaics at their glittering best.

If you want to avoid the crowds, plan to visit first thing in the morning (9.30am is the earliest time that non-worshippers are allowed inside) or in the late afternoon when daytrippers and tour groups have gone. Free tours in various languages are conducted throughout the months of July and August, beginning at 10.30pm and departing regularly until 4pm. For details, enquire at the desk to the left of the narthex.

PALAZZO DUCALE

For around nine centuries, this appropriately magnificent palace was the seat of the republic, acting as council chamber, law court and prison as well as the residence of most of Venice's doges. It remains almost exactly as it must have been 400 years ago, rich in reminders of the power that was once exercised from here.

The Doges' Palace was first built in fortress-like Byzantine style in the 9th century and partially replaced some 500 years later by a Gothic structure. (The two windows on the lagoon side which are set lower indicate the 14th-century construction.) The ravages inflicted by three devastating fires meant some extensive reconstruction work. The result is a unique and breathtaking combination of Byzantine, Gothic and Renaissance styles.

The palace's singular and quite outstanding 15th-century entranceway is called the Porta della Carta (Paper Gate). The derivation of the name is contested; for some, it refers to the fact that the doge's decrees were affixed here, to others, it relates to the nearby location of the state archives.

Just to the left, note the four curious dark brown figures of the Tetrarchs (also known as the Four Moors), variously said to represent either Diocletian and associates, or four Saracen robbers who tried to loot the basilica's treasury through the wall behind them.

Sculpted in the 4th century, this strange ensemble was removed from Acre as yet another Venetian war souvenir.

35

Inside the courtyard is the impressive ceremonial stairway, the **Scala dei Giganti**, named after Sansovino's colossal statues of Neptune and Mars, symbolizing respectively Venice's sea and land power. Tourists use the (only slightly less glamorous) gilded **Scala d'Oro**, another 16th-century creation by Jacopo Sansovino.

The doges' private quarters are often used for temporary exhibitions (usually included in the ticket price) and during these times they are sectioned off from the rest of the palace. Most are empty chambers with

fine ceilings, magnificent fireplaces and the occasional noteworthy painting.

The beautifully decorated rooms in which the business of the *Serenissima* was conducted begin in the **Anti-Collegio**. Here, pick up a portable recorder which provides a commentary of the main points of interest in each room, since there are no organized guided tours of the entire palace.

Once past the Anti-Collegio, which is adorned with Paolo Veronese's magnificent *Rape of Europa* and Jacopo Tintoretto's *Bacchus and Ariadne*,

The four enigmatic characters who stand by the entrance of the Doges' Palace.

visitors proceed to the Sala del Collegio, where the doge received ambassadors. Next is the Sala del Senato where the Venetian ruling council (made up of the doge, his advisors, members of the judiciary and senators) formulated policy.

The next room is the **Sala del Consiglio dei Deici** – the meeting room of the Council of Ten (see p.15). The Ten (who actually numbered up to 17) were a high-ranking group who met on matters of state security and acquired a Gestapo-like reputation. A letter-box in the form of a lion's mouth, for the use of citizens who wished to inform the Ten of anything untoward, can be seen in the next room. A door in the corner of this room leads to the prisons. This route can only be taken as part of a special tour known as the *Itinerari Segreti* (the Secret Route), a route that takes you through a number of rooms not open to the general public, including the torture chamber (in reality far less gruesome than it sounds) and the cell from which the infamous Casanova, another Venetian son, escaped in 1775. Tours arc conducted (in Italian only) on a daily basis except Wednesday, and are recommended. Pre-booking is necessary; for details, telephone 522 49 51.

Back on the public route, the palace's rather menacing aura is confirmed by a splendid private **armoury**, which displays some unique and very artistic deadly devices. Children (and adults) will find it all rather fascinating. **37**

The most resplendent room of all, however, is the **Sala del Maggior Consiglio** (or Great Council Chamber), a vast hall where, in the early days of democracy, Venice's citizens assembled to elect doges and argue out state policies. Later, only the nobles convened here. The hall was built to hold an assembly of up to 1,700, but by the mid-16th century this figure had increased to around 2,500. Fortunately, a full house was a rare event.

Covering the whole of one end wall is Tintoretto's *Paradise*, a monumental work based on Dante's *Paradiso* undertaken by the artist (with the assistance of his son) while he was in his seventies. At 7m by 22m (23ft by 72ft), it is the largest Old Master oil painting in the world and contains some 350 human figures.

The portraits of 76 doges, several no more than artistic guesswork, line the cornice beneath the ceiling. Conspicuous by his absence is one 14th-century doge, Marin Faliero. A black veil marks his intended place of honour and a notice tells us that he was beheaded for treason in 1355.

Pass through narrow corridors and across the legendary **Ponte dei Sospiri** (Bridge of Sighs), built in 1603, and recall the lines written by Lord Byron, 'I stood in Venice on the Bridge of Sighs; A palace and a prison on each hand.' As you will discover when recrossing this Baroque stone bridge, it has two parallel passageways, presumably so that prisoners on their way to the Council of Ten would not meet those who had already been interrogated. The name seems to derive more from romantic fiction than hard fact, as only petty criminals would have made this journey. You can see the small dark cells in which they were kept, but don't expect grisly torture machines; by the standards of medieval dungeons, they were relatively civilized.

THE PIAZZETTA

If the Piazza is Venice's drawing room, then the Piazzetta is its vestibule. The two soaring **columns** of granite were stolen from the East and hoisted upright here in 1172. They have not budged since, but a third column apparently fell into the sea, never to be recovered.

On top of one of the columns is Venice's original patron saint, St Theodore. On the other stands what must be the strangest looking of the city's many stone lions (you can see it most clearly from the balcony of the Doges' Palace). Its exact origin is unknown, but it is thought to be of Eastern provenance and may be up to 2,200 years old. It really isn't a lion at all but a *chimera*, a mythical hybrid beast, simply 'lionized' by the Venetians.

The area between the columns today bustles with tourists, but between the 15th and mid-18th centuries this was a place of execution. One of the more creative punishments for treason involved torture and burning on a raft, then being dragged through the streets by a horse before finally being put to death between the columns.

The lavish building opposite the Doges' Palace could almost be a fourth wing of the Piazza;

it even has its own café and orchestra. It is in fact the **Libreria Sansoviniana**, widely held to be Jacopo Sansovino's finest achievement. Built in 1537-91, adorned with wonderful columns and sculptures, it houses the National Library and the Old Library. The latter is closed to the general public and the

Symbol of romance throughout the world, the Bridge of Sighs has a rather less glorious history.

former is open to readers only, but you can have a look inside its porch, dominated by two giant statues. The building also houses the Museo Archeologico (see p.41).

If in need of a break from sightseeing and crowds, the secretive **Giardinetti Reali** (Royal Gardens), a few yards behind the Library, offer delicious shade. Close to the Gardens, in Palazzetto Selva, is the **tourist information office**.

MUSEUMS OF THE PIAZZA

There are two museums on the square, both of which are comparatively free of crowds. The **Museo Correr** (closed Tuesdays) is the city museum and contains something on virtually every aspect of Venice. Dedicated history students should make this a priority (a knowledge of Italian helps in order to understand the captions), while non-specialists should be more selective and not aim to cover everything.

The highlights of the Correr are some marvellous sculptures by Canova, evocatively musty old libraries, an armoury, naval sections with wonderful globes of the old world and some fascinating artefacts giving an insight into everyday life. Don't miss the incredible stilt-like platform shoes worn by 15th-century Venetian bourgeois ladies (in order to circumvent rules on how much silk and satin they could trail, as well as to keep their skirts out of the mud).

The Museum also holds two other collections, the **Quadreria Picture Gallery** and the **Museo del Risorgimento**. The Quadreria is a superb collection of Venetian paintings from the 15th-century onwards; each room is dedicated to a different theme which is clearly captioned in several languages. The collection includes some fine paintings by lesser-known Venetian artists as well as important painters such as Giovanni Bellini and Carpaccio, and there are also some good Flemish works. The Museo del Risorgimento illustrates the history of Venice from the 19th century onwards and is bound to appeal to all knowledgeable art enthusiasts.

The **Museo Archeologico** is a forgotten corner of the Piazza (it's actually off the Piazza), housing some delightful examples of classical Greek and Roman sculpture. There is even an Egyptian mummies room which is worth a look.

Museum and Art Gallery Highlights
(See also Venice Highlights on p.25)

State museums (the Accademia, Museo Orientale, Museo Archeologico and Franchetti Gallery) open 9am-2pm, Tuesday-Sunday. Check times with tourist information or in *Un Ospite di Venezia* (see p.128). The nearest *vaporetto* stop is in brackets.

Ca'd'Oro, Grand Canal, Cannaregio (*Ca'd'Oro*). Venetian Renaissance art. 9am-2pm daily (see pp.41 and 85).

Museo Correr, Ala Napoleonica, Piazza San Marco (*San Marco*). Museum of the city and Venetian art from the 13th to 16th centuries. Open Wednesday-Monday 10am-4pm (Nov-Mar), 10am-5pm (Apr-Oct) (see p.40).

Museo d'Arte Moderna, Ca'Pésaro, Grand Canal (*San Stae*). Modern Italian art. Open Tuesday-Sunday 10am-4pm (Nov-Mar), 10am-5pm (Apr-Oct) (see p.62).

Museo del Settecento Veneziano, Ca'Rezzonico, Grand Canal (*Ca'Rezzonico*). 18th-century Venetian paintings and furnishings. Open Saturday-Thursday 10am-4pm (Nov-Mar), 10am-5pm (Apr-Oct) (see pp.54-55).

Museo di Storia Naturale, Fondaco dei Turchi, Grand Canal (*San Stae or San Marcuola and traghetto*). Natural history. 9am-1pm Tuesday-Sunday (see p.62).

Museo Storico Navale, Riva San Biagio (*Arsenale*). Naval history. 9am-1pm Monday-Saturday (see p.45).

Museo Vetrario, Fondamente Giustinian, Murano (*Museo, Murano*). Glassware. 10am-5pm Thursday-Tuesday (see p.92).

On the Waterfront

There are few more stately waterfronts in the world than that of Venice's splendid *riva*, curving gently away from San Marco and entering the *ses-tiere* of Castello. The first section, the **Riva degli Schiavoni** (Quay of the Slavs), begins in front of the Doges' Palace and takes its name from the Dalmatian (Slav) merchants whose boats used to tie up here, laden with wares from the East. This is still a place of trade, though

less exotic, with souvenir stalls, gondola-shaped ice-cream fridges and itinerant drinks sellers lining the quay. Boats still tie up here, too: *vaporetti* at the busy stages of San Zaccaria and Riva degli Schiavoni, tugs waiting for their next big ship, and a whole fleet of gondolas.

After the Doges' Palace, the first point of interest is without doubt the Bridge of Sighs. You will have to turn your back to the waterfront but you certainly won't miss the footbridge vantage point in high season, when huge crowds make it almost impassable.

A few steps further along brings you up to the church of **La Pietà**, a handsome building with a fine ceiling painting by Giambattista Tiepolo (though in Venice such adornment is regarded almost as commonplace). What makes this church really special is that Antonio Vivaldi wrote many of his best works here while concert master from 1705 to 1740. Today, 'Vivaldi's Church', as it is referred to, is one of the city's leading classical music venues, not least because of its superb acoustics, which the great maestro Vivaldi himself may have advised on. A more or less

*T*he busy Riva degli Schiavoni, looking out from the tower of San Giorgio Maggiore.

43

permanent 'temporary' exhibition of instruments used by his orchestra is on show in a side room of the church.

Carry on past the statue of King Victor Emmanuel II, and you'll notice the crowds starting to thin out; by the time you reach the Arsenal *vaporetto* stop, a short stretch from the Doges' Palace, they will probably have dispersed completely, even in high season.

ARSENALE

This was once the greatest shipyard in the world. For 700 years before Napoleon's invasion, the republic's galleys and galleons were built here. Dante visited it and used it as the inspiration for his *Inferno*, though the Arsenal's 16,000 workers were highly respected and influential citizens, even if they did have to toil amidst seething cauldrons of boiling pitch.

Arsenale, meaning house of industry, is another of those Venetian words that have since passed into almost universal usage. The yard also passed on the idea of the conveyor belt system, as newly built galleys were fitted out by being towed simultaneously past the supply storehouses. Output was simply prodigious.

One of the yard's proudest achievements came in 1574, while Henry III of France was visiting Venice. In the time it took for the French king to get through his state banquet at the Doges' Palace, the Arsenal had constructed from scratch a fully equipped galley.

Today there's not a lot left to remind visitors of those heady and hellish days. Napoleon destroyed the Arsenal in 1797 and, although it was rebuilt by the Austrians, it ceased operations in 1917. It is now used by the navy and there is no public access. However, you can see the beautiful **entrance arch** dating largely from 1460 and guarded by a motley collection of photogenic white lions, all stolen from Greece. The two on the river side may date back to the 6th century BC.

To get inside the Arsenal you'll have to take the No. 5 *vaporetto* which cruises right through, though it doesn't stop.

There's little to see apart from a few derelict buildings and overgrown ruins.

The nearest you will get to the spirit of the age is in the excellent **Museo Storico Navale** (Naval History Museum). For many visitors the star attraction of the main building is the model of the last *Bucintoro* – the great gilded barge that was used by the doge on state occasions. There's much more than just models here, however. Whole sections of state barges and warships are featured and the museum is very well captioned. Don't miss the atmospheric annexe housed in the old **naval sheds** close to the Arsenal entrance (on the right-hand side of the river). The sheds house a dozen or more actual ships dating from more recent times and are extremely popular with children.

*T*he now derelict Arsenale was once the powerhouse behind the might of the Venetian empire.

Unless you're heading for the Biennale exhibition (see p.103) there's little of sightseeing interest past the Arsenal. It's worth coming this far, however, simply for the splendid view if you look back towards the Doges' Palace.

SCUOLA DI SAN GIORGIO DEGLI SCHIAVONI

Tucked away in the narrow sidestreets of Castello is one of the city's finest and most accessible treasures. Nowhere in Venice will you find so much spectacular painting on view in such a tiny space.

This captivating and intimate building was founded in 1451 as the guildhall of the city's Dalmatian merchants. At the beginning of the 16th century, these Slavs (*schiavoni*), prospering from trade with the East, commissioned Vittore Carpaccio to decorate their hall. His nine pictures, completed between 1502 and 1508, cover the walls of the ground-floor chapel and vividly depict the lives of the three Dalmatian patron saints – Jerome, Tryphone and George. Carpaccio's gory masterpiece of **St George and the Dragon** is particularly memorable. You will find more works on display in a side room situated off the hall and upstairs.

MORE OF SAN MARCO AND CASTELLO

If you have more time to explore this area, there are three churches and a rather intriguing tower to visit, all within a few minutes' walk of the Piazza San Marco. The tower, much photographed for city postcards but little seen by most visitors, is the **Scala del Bovolo**. Built around 1499, such graceful, spiral, external staircases were once fairly common in Venetian domestic architecture. It is open during the summer from 10.30am to 12.30pm and from 3.30 to 5.30pm. It is rather hidden away, but just follow the yellow signpost plaques, from Campo Manin.

A mere three minutes' walk east of the Piazza is the splendid early 16th-century church of **San Zaccaria**. Supposedly

the last resting place of Zaccharias (father of John the Baptist, whose body still lies in the right aisle), this Gothic-Renaissance masterpiece features a celebrated painting by Giovanni Bellini of the *Madonna and Saints* (1505), but the real treat is to discover the **side chapels**. Here you will find not only splendid glowing altarpieces but one of the most atmospheric spots in the city; an eerie and permanently flooded 8th-century **crypt**, where several early doges are interred in cool, watery graves.

Many gondolas are so well polished that you can see your face in them!

In contrast to these seldom visited spots, the churches of Santo Stefano and Santa Maria Formosa are situated on two of the area's busiest squares. The Gothic **Santo Stefano**, close to the Accademia bridge, is a large airy structure with a quiet, serene atmosphere and some rich ornamentation, including **47** paintings by Tintoretto. It's also a favourite concert venue.

The colourful square of **Santa Maria Formosa**, a short walk north-west of the Piazza, bustles with fruit and vegetable stalls while the 15th-century church contains a notable altarpiece by Palma il Vecchio amongst other worthy paintings and monuments.

Dorsoduro

'Dorsoduro' is a name with which few, if any, first-time visitors to Venice will be familiar, yet most will visit this *sestiere*, if only to see the Accademia or the church of Santa Maria della Salute. The district of Dorsoduro encompasses that portion of Venice which lies across the Grand Canal from San Marco, its eastern boundary marked by the Punta della Dogana and, to the north, by Rio Nuovo-Rio Foscari.

The eastern section as far as the area bounded by the Rio di San Sebastiano and the Rio di Santa Margherita is perhaps the most picturesque in all Venice.

This quiet residential area can boast three of the city's finest art collections as well as many excellent restaurants and shops, and benefits from the bohemian influence of the University.

THE ACCADEMIA

The Accademia is certainly the finest collection of Venetian art in existence and is the most visited spot in the city after the Piazza and the Doges' Palace. A limit of 180 visitors inside the gallery at any one time is imposed, so you should arrive early to try and avoid the inevitable queues.

The collection spans paintings from the 14th to the 19th centuries and is arranged more or less chronologically in 24 rooms. Most visitors, with only a limited amount of time to spare, can hardly expect to absorb all the riches displayed here, and it's sensible to be selective rather than trying to see everything and taking in nothing. The following brief review of the museum's highlights should help you make the most of your visit.

Venetian Artists

Venice's greatest legacy, apart from the city itself, is its painting. **Jacopo Bellini** (1400-70) and his sons **Giovanni** (1430-1516) and **Gentile** (1429-1507) inaugurated the *Serenissima*'s glorious era of art in the 15th century. The Venetian High Renaissance began with **Giorgione** (1477-1510), and three masters carried it to the supreme heights: **Titian** (1490-1576), **Jacopo Tintoretto** (1518-94) and **Paolo Veronese** (1528-88).

Titian, who was apprentice to Bellini and collaborated with Giorgione, is hailed by many as the greatest painter of his time. He is abundantly represented in Venice, and many of his masterworks – brilliantly coloured, dynamic compositions – are on display at the Frari church.

Tintoretto's works, too, can be seen all over the city but nowhere is his genius more evident than in the glowing series he painted to cover the walls and ceiling of the Scuola di San Rocco. **Veronese** has his own church, San Sebastiano, resplendent with his joyous paintings, and at the Accademia there is his monumental *Feast at the House of Levi*.

That most Venetian of painters, **Vittore Carpaccio** (1445-1526), left us intricately detailed scenes of city life between 1490 and 1526, as well as the narrative series at the Scuola di San Giorgio degli Schiavoni.

Carpaccio influenced **Antonio Canaletto** (1697-1768), whose views of Venice are reproduced endlessly today throughout the world. In the city itself, however, the artist is notable for his comparative absence. His English patron, Josef Smith, sold almost all his works abroad (mostly to England), leaving Venice with just three canvasses on show to the public – two in the Ca'Rezzonico and one in the Accademia.

Perhaps the finest Venetian decorative painter was **Giovanni Battista Tiepolo** (1696-1770), whose works are on view around Venice, but who is probably most admired for his vast paintings in the royal palace in Madrid.

Room 2 contains Carpaccio's striking *Crucifixion of the Ten Thousand Martyrs*, while Room 4 draws crowds of art lovers for its exquisite group of paintings, including Mantegna's *St George* and a fine series of works by Giovanni Bellini and Giorgione.

Room 5 holds the gallery's most famous piece, Giorgione's *Tempest*, and in Room 10 is Veronese's much discussed *Feast at the House of Levi*, a compelling canvas illustrating The Last Supper which covers an entire wall. In the same room hang Jacopo Tintoretto's dazzling St Mark paintings, notably the haunting *Transport of the Body of St Mark*. Also in room 5, Titian's dark and sober *Pietà* (his own obituary work, unfinished at the time of his death) is worth lingering over. So too is room 11, which contains some ovewhelming works of art: Veronese and Tintoretto masterpieces as well as some memorable Tiepolos.

As for room 17, it contains a Venetian rarity – a painting by Canaletto, the Accademia's only work by the artist.

Out of sequence, room 23 is housed in the top of the church which constitutes part of the gallery structure. The airy, spacious loft is the perfect setting for some splendid altarpieces, notably the faded but still powerful *Blessed Lorenzo Giustinian*, by Gentile Bellini.

Room 20, however, is probably the most stunning of the Accademia, with four immense paintings occupying one wall apiece. Gentile Bellini's celebrated *Procession Around the Piazza Bearing the Cross* reveals how little San Marco has changed since 1496, except for its mosaics and the addition of the clock tower and Procuratie Nuove. Other illustrious paintings in room 20 include Carpaccio's epic *The Miracle of the Holy Cross at the Rialto Bridge*, showing the old bridge at the Rialto (see p.58) and intriguingly familiar gondolas on the Grand Canal.

Carpaccio's greatly admired *St Ursula* cycle is in room 21. It depicts events from the tragic heroine's life, from acceptance of the hand of the British prince, Hereus, in return for his conversion to Christianity to their subsequent pilgrimage to Rome and their eventual martyrdom at the hands of heathen Attila the Hun.

COLLEZIONE GUGGENHEIM

A few yards away from the Accademia is another splendid gallery, regarded as one of the best and most comprehensive collections of modern art in Europe. The bequest of American expatriate and heiress Peggy Guggenheim, who died in 1979, is displayed in her home, the partially built 18th-century Palazzo Venier dei Leoni, overlooking the Grand Canal.

Among the outstanding exhibits are Picasso's charming *La Baignade* and Constantine Brancusi's bronze sculpture, *Bird in Space*. Other highlights include works by Marcel Duchamp, Max Ernst, Dalí, Miró, Piet Mondrian and American Jackson Pollock.

You're unlikely to miss the bold bronze equestrian statue facing the Grand Canal. The curator has referred to Marino Marini's *Angel of the City* as the collection's 'pride and joy', but on occasions the gates onto the water have been closed because of repeated complaints from prudish onlookers offended by the naked statue's frankness. More Guggenheim wit is on display elsewhere: look out for the brightly painted metal crocodiles on the mooring posts in the canal. The Palazzo Venier is closed on Tuesday.

Another important art museum is the **Collezione Cini**, open during the summer and located just a short distance away between the Guggenheim and the Accademia.

SANTA MARIA DELLA SALUTE

The truly magnificent Baroque church of Santa Maria della Salute is almost as familiar a Venetian landmark as the Basilica or Doges' Palace. Indeed, the octagonal structure has presided over the entrance to the Grand Canal for longer than 300 years.

Santa Maria della Salute was built as a thanksgiving to the **51**

Virgin Mary for the end of a catastrophic plague in 1630 which wiped out nearly one in three of the lagoon's inhabitants. In fact, the Salute was not completed until 1682 – the fifty-year dream of architect Baldassare Longhena – and was erected on more than one million sunken oak pilings, each 3.5m (12ft) long. Since 1670 Venice has been celebrating the Festa della Salute on 21 November; every year, engineers build a great pontoon of boats over the Grand Canal and most of the city's population, resident and visiting, walk across the water and into the church. Only on this day are its main doors open.

Inside, in the sacristy to the left of the high altar, hangs Tintoretto's great *Marriage at Cana*. A number of Titians and a *Madonna* by Palma il Vecchio can also be seen.

The Santa Maria della Salute and neighbouring palazzi provide a suitably majestic entrance to the Grand Canal.

THE DOGANA AND ZATTERE

Continue east from the Salute towards the wedge-shaped tip of Dorsoduro which marks the end of the Grand Canal to discover the 17th-century **Dogana di Mare** (Customs House). At the tip of its tower is the curious balletic wind-vane entitled **statue of Fortune** (but also possibly Justice) holding a ship's rudder, set on a large golden globe supported by two Atlas-like figures.

The **view** from here, looking straight into St Mark's Basin in one direction and across the lagoon in the other, is one of the most breathtaking in all the city. Here begins the Fondamenta delle Zattere, a long quay which runs along the waterfront all the way to the Rio di San Sebastiano.

The floating rafts which gave the Zattere its name were once major unloading points for cargoes of salt and other valuable commodities. The only floating rafts you'll see these days are used by restaurants or the local rowing club. **53**

The huge salt warehouse, which was once capable of storing over 40,000 tons of the precious mineral, is now partly used by a canoe club. Look out across the Giudecca Canal to the inner island suburb of Giudecca for a fine view of the **Redentore** (Redeemer) church, designed by Palladio. This was built, like the Salute after it, as an act of thanksgiving at the end of a terrible plague epidemic in 1575-76. There is an annual celebration here too, on the third Sunday of July, which involves a frantic boat-pontoon crossing and culminates in a spectacular firework display.

Continue along the Zattere past the churches of Spirito Santo and the Gesuati (Santa Maria del Rosario). Turn right onto the Fondamente Nani, and a few yards further along on the opposite side you will see the attractive **Squero di San Trovaso**. *Squero* means boatyard – a common component of Venetian street terminology, as you may already have noticed. Only a handful of *squeri* are still in operation in Venice today and San Trovaso is the only yard where you can see gondolas and other craft which are waiting to be repaired.

The area around San Trovaso is utterly charming and you may decide to ignore the remainder of your day's planned itinerary simply to wander at random in the cool streets and alleys. The church of San Trovaso is worth investigating for two of Tintoretto's last works, both completed by his son.

If you do make your way back to the Zattere, the huge red-brick landmark you can see across the water right at the western end of Giudecca is the **Molino Stucky** (Stucky's Mill) – a flour mill which took its present shape in the 1890s and earned a fortune for the eponymous Signor Stucky before finally closing down in 1954. It has remained deserted ever since.

CA'REZZONICO

The Ca'Rezzonico, also known as the Museo del Settecento Veneziano (Museum of 18th-century Venice), contains the third of Dorsoduro's important art and museum collections. Here, however, the 17th-century palatial setting is at least as important as the 18th-century exhibits it harbours.

Stepping into the Ca' Rezzonico is a veritable feast for the eyes. First, a stunning ballroom awaits you at the top of the vast entrance staircase. It features two splendid and immense Murano glass chandeliers and vibrantly colourful ceilings and walls. In the adjacent room are some intricately carved figures of chained slaves.

Ceilings by Tiepolo (father and son) are the main artistic interest until you reach the gallery on the second floor. Here the works of Pietro Longhi are highly regarded and most visitors are immediately drawn to the two **Canaletto paintings** of the Grand Canal (surprisingly, the only two such views by the artist to be found on public display in the city).

O*n the Zattere, admire the sober interior of the church of Santa Maria del Rosario Gesuati.*

Upstairs, on the third floor, don't miss the old, quaint puppet theatre and an interesting reproduction of an 18th-century pharmacy. The view from the windows along the Grand Canal is also to be savoured.

Incidentally, the poet Robert Browning passed away in an apartment of the palace (not open to the public) in 1889 and his son, Pen, owned the palace for a while during the 19th century. The American-born artist James Whistler also lived here in 1879-80. The museum is open daily except Friday.

THE 'UNIVERSITY QUARTER'

The attractive area around the Campo di Santa Margherita, bounded by the canals of Rio Foscari, Rio di Santa Margherita and Rio di San Barnaba, is pervaded (but not dominated) by the bohemian atmosphere of the university.

Along the Grand Canal, a short distance from Ca'Rezzonico, is the main university building of Ca'Foscari. Do take time, however, to walk along the side of the Rio di San Barnaba, where you'll see the picturesque fruit and vegetable barges moored along the quay.

The **Campo di Santa Margherita** is in term time the liveliest square in Venice outside the Piazza. It houses numerous cheap restaurants and some alternative shops as well as colourful market stalls. The church of Santa Margherita is currently being restored but at the other end of the square look in at the **Carmini** (Carmelite Order) church where a spacious interior holds some grandiose galleries and plenty of visual interest. For more religious art, call in next door at the **Scuola Grande dei Carmini** to admire the fine ceiling paintings by Giambattista Tiepolo.

San Polo and Santa Croce

The two *sestieri* of San Polo and Santa Croce cover the northern half of the left bank of the Grand Canal. In the interests of simplification, we have referred to the entire area as San Polo, since that is the largest and most important district of the two. It encompasses many important sights, including the artistic treasure houses of the Frari and the Scuola Grande di San Rocco, as well as one of the city's most colourful attractions, the famous Rialto markets.

THE RIALTO

Rialto, derived from *Rivo Alto* (high bank), was settled by the first Venetians in the 9th century. Ever since then, this district, which covers both sides of the Grand Canal (straddling San Polo and San Marco), has been the city's commercial hub. During the peak of the republic's influence it was one of the most important financial centres in Europe, as reflected in *The Merchant of Venice* when Shylock asks of Bassanio 'What news on the Rialto?'. Less grandly, the area was also renowned throughout Europe for its brothels.

Today, most of the banks and all of the bordellos have gone, but there are still traders in full cry. On the old **Rialto Bridge** (*Ponte di Rialto*), and spilling over into San Polo, you will find all manner of shops, ranging from high-class jewellers, clothing and shoe shops to the cheapest trinket vendors.

*T*he Rialto Bridge – once said to be the finest single arch in Europe – has been the city's main river crossing point for over 400 years.

The bridge itself succeeded three earlier wooden structures, all destroyed by fire. It was thus constructed of Istrian stone in the 16th century and remained, until the mid-19th century, the only crossing point over the Grand Canal (see p.64).

What makes the Rialto really worth visiting is Venice's principle **market**, concentrated around a few tiny alleyways and on the quayside area to the right-hand side as you cross the bridge. Here, at the *erberia* (fruit and vegetable market) and *pescheria* (fish market), housewives, chefs and servants have been buying their daily supplies since 1097. This marvellous, colourful and animated spectacle is the best free show in Venice; the markets are open every morning apart from Sunday and holidays.

Aside from the market stalls you will find some of Venice's most tempting food shops and characterful bars. **Do Mori** on Calle do Mori is a city legend – a dark place, its ceiling crammed with brass pots, it serves excellent *cicheti* (see p.109) and cheap wine to market traders and tourists in the know. One way or another, you're most unlikely to go hungry in this particular area.

CAMPO DI SAN POLO

This is the biggest *campo* in the city outside the Piazza and is notable for its church and the late 14th- to mid-15th-century **Palazzo Soranzo**. There's no public entry to this attractive, reddish-coloured palace, but you can't miss it as it's the largest building on the square opposite the church. There's no plaque to tell you so, but Casanova once lived here.

Note the fine main doorway of the **church of San Polo**, one of the few features that survives from the original 15th-century building. The dark interior is reached through a side door and features a brooding *Last Supper* by Tintoretto.

The campanile, dating from 1362, stands a short way across the church of San Polo and is adorned with two of the republic's less friendly lions, one playing with a human head, the other with a serpent.

THE FRARI

Santa Maria Gloriosa dei Frari (known simply as the Frari, a deformation of *frati*, meaning brothers) is Venice's second church after San Marco. The 'brothers' in question are of the Franciscan order, who were granted a piece of land in 1236. The church was built between 1340 and 1469. It is a huge, lofty structure, rather imposing from the outside but bright and airy inside, and a suitably impressive setting for some considerable art treasures.

A modest entrance fee is charged, and the back of the ticket shows an excellent plan of the church's principal highlights. Proceeding by this plan, turn left on entering the church and continue your visit in a clockwise direction.

The Frari's greatest treasure is Titian's brilliant *Assumption*, painted in 1518, taking pride of place above the high altar. To the right of this (No. 14 on the ticket plan) is Donatello's much-admired statue of *St John the Baptist*, its glowing colours having been restored in the 19th century. This wooden piece is the Florentine artist's sole remaining work in Venice. Also in this part of the church, tucked away in the sacristy (No. 19) is the *Madonna and Saints* (1488) – a triptych masterpiece by Giovanni Bellini,

T he start of the fruit and vegetable market, by the Church of San Giacomo di Rialto.

*P*ride of the Frari – Titian's exuberant Assumption is a highlight of the Master's illustrious career.

posite sides of the great nave. Titian was buried here in 1576 but the monument was not built until the mid-19th century. Canova's mausoleum was erected in 1827, five years after his death, but only his heart is interred here.

Several doges are also entombed in the Frari (two are in the high altar) and one of the city's most bombastic monuments can be found here (next to Canova), dedicated to Doge Giovanni Pésaro.

Just before you leave the church, note the splendid *Madonna di Ca'Pésaro* by Titian (No. 4), which is thought to represent the artist's wife.

which many visitors actually prefer to the better known *Assumption*. Finally in this area, don't miss the beautiful marquetry and intricate carving on the choir stalls.

The Frari is also notable for its huge monuments to Titian (Tiziano) and Canova on op-

THE SCUOLA GRANDE DI SAN ROCCO

The Scuola Grande di San Rocco stirs the emotions. John Ruskin, the foremost art historian of the 19th century and possibly the city's most scrupulous observers, described it as one of the three most precious picture collections in all Italy (ranking it above the Accademia). Henry James was also a devotee, but he found it breathtaking in more ways than one, his ultimate verdict being that it was 'suffocating'.

San Rocco, formerly one of the five great Venetian *scuole* (craft guilds and confraternities of laymen under the banner of a particular saint), commissioned Tintoretto to decorate the interior in 1564, and for 15 of the next 23 years much of his time was spent painting the 65 pictures here. (In addition, there are a few works by other Venetian masters.)

Tintoretto began upstairs in the sumptuous **Sala dell'Albergo**, just off the main hall, so make your way there directly before coming back down to the lower hall. His monumental *Crucifixion* (described by Ruskin as 'beyond all analysis and above all praise') is said to have been considered by the artist his greatest painting.

In the dimly lit main hall, the gloriously gilded **ceiling** is covered with 21 immense pictures and there are another 13 on the walls (fear not, all are captioned on the helpful plan provided free at the entrance).

The best way of studying the sacred ceiling works is to find a mirror and focus on the detail, rather than attempting to take in broad sweeps at once. Hidden in the gloom beneath the murals are some marvellous, if odd, wooden figures by Venice's off-beat 17th-century sculptor, Francesco Pianto.

In contrast to the main hall, the pictures in the ground floor hall seem almost light and airy. They represent scenes from the life of the Virgin. Look out particularly for *The Flight into Egypt*, acknowledged as another of Tintoretto's finest paintings. More Tintorettos are on display in the Church of San Rocco next door.

MUSEUMS OF SAN POLO

Close to Campo San Polo and the Frari is the **Casa Museo di Goldoni**, the house in which Carlo Goldoni (see p.9) was born in 1707. This 'large and beautiful house set between the Nomboli and Donna Onesta Bridges' was turned in 1952 into a museum dedicated to the **61** prolific playwright of the *commedia dell'arte* school. During the summer you may come across some of his plays being performed outdoors in the larger city squares. The museum is small and its theatrical memorabilia will probably appeal only to specialists. However, it is worth visiting for the opportunity of seeing inside a well-preserved Gothic palace and in particular for its handsome courtyard. The Casa Museo di Goldoni is open from 8.30am until 1.30pm only; it is closed all day Sunday.

The district's other two museums are situated to the north, both on the Grand Canal. Santa Stae is the nearest *vaporetto* stage. Lovers of modern art and samurai costumes should turn left, those interested in natural history should turn right.

The **Museo d'Arte Moderna** (Museum of Modern Art), housed in the Ca'Pésaro (see p.81), was founded with the best of the Biennale exhibition pieces (see p.103) and features Italian artists for the most part, although a few important international contemporary works are also represented. Above it in the same building is located the **Museo Orientale** (Oriental Museum), a rather confusing jumble of lacquered pieces, samurai arms and armour, and other Eastern artefacts. Both the Arte Moderna and Orientale are closed on Monday.

The **Museo di Storia Naturale** (Natural History Museum) has a rather old-fashioned collection, though it is a popular choice with children. Among the more terrifying exhibits are a monster crab with legs reaching a full 2m (6ft) and a scorpion over 30cm (1ft) long. The most impressive exhibits, however, are to be found in the Dinosaur Room, which features the awesome bones of possibly the largest extinct crocodilian creatures ever found (measuring 11m/37ft in length) and the complete skeleton of a massive biped reptile known as an *Ouranosaurus* (standing at almost 3.6m/12ft high and some 7m or 23ft long). Both came from the Sahara.

The museum of Natural History is open in the morning only, and is closed on Monday.

The Grand Canal

Difficult as it is for a visitor accustomed to cars and asphalt to get used to the idea, this unforgettable waterway is actually the main street of Venice. Visitors know it as the Grand Canal but to the Venetians it is the *canalazzo*, stretching over 4km (2 miles) from inauspicious beginnings near the railway station to a glorious final outpouring into St Mark's Basin. The canal is so compellingly beautiful that many visitors ride the *vaporetti* back and forth for hours, just taking in the spectacular views. Embark on the No. 1, the inappropriately named *accelerato*, which stops at every landing stage!

No matter where you are in Venice, waterside dining is never far away. The restaurants along the Grand Canal are the most popular.

The banks of the canal are lined with over 200 ornate palaces (*palazzi*) and grand houses, mostly built between the 14th and 18th centuries. Some have been superbly restored, while others have a neglected air, awaiting their turn in the endless queue for renovation. Few are still inhabited by the aristocratic families for whom they were built. Instead, most have been turned into municipal offices and hotels, or museums and exhibition galleries.

Here are some of the most outstanding palaces to look for while travelling from the railway station towards the Piazza San Marco along the canal. Unless otherwise noted, there is no public access.

THE LEFT BANK

The first house of note is the **Palazzo Vendramin-Calergi** (dating from the early 16th century), a large classical-style building where Richard Wagner once had rooms. The building now provides a more than suitably opulent setting for Venice's winter casino.

The **Ca'd'Oro** (built 1425-c.1440) is perhaps the most famous frontage on the Grand Canal and certainly boasts the most elaborate Gothic façade, as well as some of the most beautiful tracery in the city. Its name (House of Gold) comes from its once gilded sculptures. Unfortunately, the front is undergoing restoration and is likely to remain boarded up for the foreseeable future. However, you can visit the interior which holds a fine collection of paintings and sculptures (see p.85).

Shortly before reaching the Rialto, the Venetian-Byzantine-style **Ca'da Mosto** (13th century) is one of the oldest houses on the canal. The landmark **Rialto Bridge** was designed by the aptly named Antonio da Ponte in 1588, who beat off proposals by Sansovino, Palladio and Michelangelo.

If you want to walk or dine alongside the canal, this is the place to do it. Much of the rest of the banks are inaccessible.

The handsome twin *palazzi* of **Loredan** and **Farsetti** (dating from the 13th century) now function as the town hall.

Hotels and Restaurants in Venice

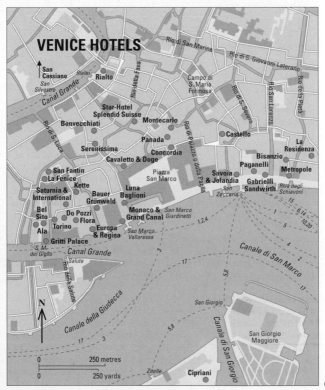

VENICE HOTELS

Rio di San Marina
Rio di S. Giovanni Laterano
Rio de la Pietà
Rio di San Severo
San Cassiano
Rialto
San Silvestro
Rialto
Canal Grande
Rio della Fava
Campo di S. Maria Formosa
Rio di Palazzo o della Paglia
Rio di S. Lorenzo
Star-Hotel Splendid Suisse
Bonvecchiati
Montecarlo
Castello
La Residenza
Rio di S. Luca
Panada
Serenissima
Concordia
Bisanzio
Metropole
Cavaletto & Doge
Paganelli
San Fantin
Piazza San Marco
La Fenice
Savoia & Jolandia
Kette
Gabrielli
Saturnia & International
Bauer
Luna Baglioni
Sandwirth
Grünwald
San Zaccaria
Riva degli Schiavoni
Bel Sito
Do Pozzi
Monaco & Grand Canal
San Marco Giardinetti
Flora
Torino
15
Ala
Europa & Regina
San Marco Vallaresso
6,14
Gritti Palace
1,2,4
10,20
S. M. del Giglio
5
Canal Grande
Salute
3
Canale di San Marco
Rio della Salute
17
17
Canale della Giudecca
5,8
N
San Giorgio
17
3
5,8
Canale di San Giorgio
San Giorgio Maggiore
0   250 metres
0   250 yards
Zitelle
Cipriani

65

Recommended Hotels

Below is a selection of hotels in different price bands. Venice is nearly always busy so book early, particularly in high season. The star rating in brackets after each hotel name refers to its official government grading (see p.116).

As a guide to room prices, we have used the following symbols to denote the price of a double room with bath or shower per night, including breakfast and tax, during high season, from spring to autumn. Carnival and Christmas week are also very popular times of the year.

▓▓▓▓	L.400,000 and above
▓▓▓	L.250-400,000
▓▓	L.165-250,000
▓	L.100-165,000

SAN MARCO AND CASTELLO

Ala (3-star) ▓▓
Campo Santa Maria del Giglio
Tel. 520 83 33
Fax 520 63 90
An historic house, renovated with traditionally decorated public areas and modern bedrooms. Wheelchair access. 77 rooms.

Bauer Grünwald & Grand Hotel (4-star de luxe) ▓▓▓▓
Campo San Moisè
Tel. 520 70 22
Fax 520 75 57
The landside extension of this hotel is one of Venice's few modern intrusions and stands out as a result; the Grand Canal side, however, reveals a rather splendid 13th-century palace. The hotel contains beautiful traditionally furnished rooms. Wheelchair access. 214 rooms.

Bel Sito & Berlino (3-star) ▓▓
Campo Santa Maria del Giglio
Tel. 522 33 65
Fax 520 40 83
In this very friendly small hotel, bedrooms are furnished in a pleasant, traditional 18th-19th-century style. Rear-facing rooms are particularly recommended, because they tend to be quieter. Wheelchair access. 34 rooms.

Bisanzio   ‖
(3-star)
Calle della Pietà
off Riva degli Schiavoni
Tel. 520 31 00
Fax 520 41 14
This small modern hotel is situated in a peaceful spot just off the bustling Riva degli Schiavoni, or Quay of the Slavs (see p.42). 40 simply furnished modern and traditional bedrooms.

Bonvecchiati   ‖-‖‖‖
(3-star)
Calle Goldoni
Tel. 528 50 17
Fax 528 52 30
The Bonvecchiati Hotel occupies an old house, recently renovated and fitted in a grand style with a tasteful blend of antique and reproduction furniture. Very close to the Piazza San Marco. 86 rooms.

Castello   ‖
(3-star)
Calle Sacrestia, off Campo Santi Filippo e Giacomo
Tel. 523 02 17
Fax 521 10 23
The Castello is a small, cosy hotel situated right by a lively square. The rooms are all modern, and some are decorated with traditional Italian furnishings. Wheelchair access. 26 rooms.

Cavalletto & Doge   ‖‖‖
Orseolo
(4-star)
San Marco
Tel. 520 09 55
Fax 523 81 84
Situated just off the Piazza San Marco and backing onto a main gondola mooring basin, this five-storey hotel is rather old-fashioned and staid, but does offer spacious rooms. 81 rooms.

Concordia   ‖‖‖
(4-star)
Calle Larga San Marco
Tel. 520 68 66
Fax 520 67 75
The only hotel actually to look onto the Piazza, the Concordia offers some absolutely splendid views from its rooftop dining area. The rooms are spacious and traditionally furnished. Wheelchair access. 53 rooms.

Do Pozzi   ‖
(3-star)
Corte dei do Pozzi
off Calle Larga 22 Marzo
Tel. 520 78 55
Fax 522 94 13
An old house, recently renovated, hidden away on a small square where breakfast is taken in summer. Pleasant public rooms, 29 modern and functional bedrooms. **67**

Recommended Hotels

Europa & Regina ▐▐▐▐
(4-star de luxe)

San Marco
Tel. 520 04 77
Fax 523 15 33

A renowned CIGA/Sheraton property on the Grand Canal enjoying a splendid position and some spectacular terrace views opposite the church of Santa Maria della Salute (see p.51). 189 rooms.

La Fenice et ▐▐
des Artistes
(3-star)

Campiello Fenice
Tel. 523 23 33
Fax 520 37 21

La Fenice et des Artistes is set in an old house next to the theatre of the same name (see p.102). The rooms are decorated with a mixture of antique and modern furnishings, and there is also a pleasant terrace garden. 65 rooms.

Flora ▐▐
(3-star)

Off Calle Larga 22 Marzo
Tel. 520 58 44
Fax 522 82 17

Flora is a beautiful small hotel where all public areas and bedrooms are in traditional style. Another advantage is the delightful secluded rear garden. Wheelchair access. 44 rooms.

Gabrielli Sandwirth ▐▐▐
(4-star)

Riva degli Schiavoni
Tel. 523 15 80
Fax 520 94 55

Set in a Gothic palace with fine views over the lagoon and waterfront. In summer meals are served in the pretty courtyard and guests may enjoy the rooftop sun-lounge and rose-garden. 100 rooms.

Gritti Palace ▐▐▐▐
(5-star de luxe)

Campo Santa Maria del Giglio
Tel. 79 46 11
Fax 520 09 42

Housed in a 15th-century doge's palace looking out onto the Grand Canal, the CIGA/Sheraton-owned Gritti Palace offers the last word in traditional grandeur. The rooms are beautifully furnished. Wheelchair access. 88 rooms.

Kette ▐▐
(3-star)

Piscina San Moisè
Tel. 520 77 66
Fax 522 89 64

This hotel is set in a beautifully renovated old house with lots of polished wood and warm mellow furnishings extending to the bedrooms. It is particularly popular with tour groups. Wheelchair access. 44 rooms.

Luna Hotel   ▌▌▌-▌▌▌▌
Baglioni
(4-star)

Calle Larga dell'Ascensione
Tel. 528 98 40
Fax 528 71 60
Grand hotel with five-star aspirations as well as an historic pedigree, though much modernized. Splendid public rooms and traditionally furnished rooms. Wheelchair access. 130 rooms.

Metropole   ▌▌▌▌
(4-star)

Riva degli Schiavoni
Tel. 520 50 44
Fax 522 36 79
This early-19th-century house, set on the main quay, has been sympathetically restored and abounds in antiques and other curious collectibles. The rooms are traditionally decorated; the service is excellent. 64 rooms.

Monaco & Grand   ▌▌▌▌
Canal (4-star)

Calle Vallaresso
Tel 520 02 11
Fax 520 05 01
An atmospheric 18th-century palace with five-star views complementing its many other grand trimmings. The bedrooms are decorated in a tastefully restrained modern-traditional style. 75 rooms.

Montecarlo   ▌▌
(3-star)

Calle dei Specchieri
Tel. 520 71 44
Fax 520 77 89
The Montecarlo is a small modern hotel, set in a busy thoroughfare off the Piazza San Marco (the bedrooms are soundproofed, however, so relatively quiet). Wheelchair access. 48 rooms.

Paganelli   ▌
(2-star)

Riva degli Schiavoni
Tel. 522 43 24
Fax 523 92 67
A small hotel with simple but adequate rooms, benefitting from the same waterfront viewpoint as its grander and more expensive competitors (when booking, specify room facing onto the lagoon). Wheelchair access. 15 rooms.

Panada   ▌▌
(3-star)

Calle dei Specchieri
Tel. 520 90 88
Fax 520 96 19
This modern hotel, set on a busy street off the Piazza San Marco, is tastefully decorated in a mixture of modern and old Venetian styles. Good service, and convenient and friendly pub-like bar. Wheelchair access. 46 rooms.

69

Pensione Bucintoro (2-star)

Riva degli Schiavoni
Tel. 522 32 40
Fax 523 52 24

The *pensione*'s bedrooms are very simply furnished, in modern style, but all enjoy splendid views over the lagoon and along the waterfront towards San Marco. The pleasant breakfast room is a definite plus point. 28 rooms.

Pensione Wildner (2-star)

Riva degli Schiavoni
Tel. 522 74 63
Fax 526 56 15

The Pensione Wildner is a fairly basic but comfortable small hotel and restaurant offering wonderful views over to the island of San Giorgio Maggiore (see p.89) and the lagoon. 19 rooms.

La Residenza (2-star)

Campo Bandiera e Moro
Tel. 528 53 15
Fax 523 88 59

A most remarkable 14th-century palace, complete with 18th-century frescos, La Residenza is set on a pleasant, quiet square. The hotel may not rank highly on modern comforts, the atmosphere more than compensates. 17 rooms.

Rialto (3-star)

Riva del Ferro
Tel. 520 91 66
Fax 523 89 58

This hotel benefits from a splendid location, adjacent – as its name indicates – to the Rialto Bridge, (very central, if you don't mind the endless stream of tourists gathering in this prime spot). Spectacular views along the Grand Canal. Modern bedroom décor. Wheelchair access. 76 rooms.

San Fantin (2-star)

Campiello Fenice
Tel. 523 14 01

The San Fantin is a tiny hotel with a curious stone façade, set in a pleasant quiet location, very close to the pretty La Fenice theatre (see p.102). The interior is modest and modern. 14 rooms.

San Marco (3-star)

Ponte dei Dai
Tel. 520 42 77
Fax 523 84 47

This is a small hotel set on one of the busy San Marco-Rialto principal thoroughfares. The hotel is particularly popular with both large groups and tour operators. 57 modern functional bedrooms.

Saturnia & International (4-star)

𝄇𝄇𝄇𝄇

Calle Larga 22 Marzo
Tel. 520 83 77
Fax 520 71 31
Built around a 14th-century doge's palace, this hotel has been run by the same family since 1908. Request a room in the old part. Two outstanding restaurants. Wheelchair access. 102 rooms.

Savoia & Jolandia (3-star)

𝄇𝄇

Riva degli Schiavoni
Tel. 520 66 44
Fax 520 74 94
This grand-looking establishment has many rooms with balconies looking onto the lagoon. Bedrooms decorated in simple modern style. Wheelchair access. 77 rooms.

Serenissima (2-star)

𝄇

Calle Goldoni
Tel. 520 00 11; fax 522 32 92
Pleasantly furnished small hotel conveniently situated between Rialto and the Piazza. 34 rooms.

Star-Hotel Splendid Suisse (4-star)

𝄇𝄇𝄇𝄇

Mercerie
Tel. 520 07 55; fax 528 64 98
This is a modern hotel with spacious and functional rooms and good business facilities. It also offers an attractive rooftop terrace with some views over the city. Wheelchair access. 157 rooms.

Torino (3-star)

𝄇𝄇

Calle delle Ostreghe
Tel. 520 52 22
Fax 522 82 27
The Torino is a small modern hotel set within the shell of a 15th-century palace, located on a busy thoroughfare. Simply and tastefully furnished rooms in traditional style. 20 rooms.

SAN POLO AND DORSODURO

Accademia Villa Maravege (Pensione Accademia) (3-star)

𝄇𝄇

Fondamente Bollani
Dorsoduro
Tel. 521 01 88
Fax 523 91 52
Beautiful, tranquil, small hotel set in a 17th-century villa (on a historical note, it used to be the Russian Embassy) with delightful gardens. Excellent location in the Dorsoduro district, close to the Accademia Gallery (see p.48). It is also very popular, so be sure to book well ahead. 27 rooms.

71

Agli Alboreti   I-II
(2-star)
Rio Tera Santa Agnese
Dorsoduro
Tel. 523 00 58
Fax 521 01 58
Charming, small family-run hotel
with the atmosphere of a private
house. Characterful public areas,
19 bedrooms simply and tastefully
decorated, and an excellent restaurant. Wheelchair access.

American   II
(3-star)
San Vio, Dorsoduro
Tel. 520 47 33
Fax 520 40 48
All the rooms of this small, well-
run hotel are furnished in tasteful,
traditional Venetian style. Pretty
canal-side setting. 29 rooms.

Locanda Sturion   II
(3-star)
Calle del Sturion
San Polo
Tel. 523 62 43
Fax 522 83 78
An historic building first men-
tioned in the 13th century, located
a few steps from the Rialto markets. Breakfast and reading room
overlooking the Grand Canal, and
tastefully furnished, traditional-
style bedrooms. Wheelchair access. 11 rooms.

72

Messner   I
(2-star)
Salute, Dorsoduro
Tel. 522 74 43
Fax 522 72 66
Messner is a small, well-run hotel
set on a quiet street close to the
church of Santa Maria della Salute.
There are 13 small, comfortable
bedrooms, as well as a breakfast
terrace. Wheelchair access.

Pensione Seguso   I-II
(2-star)
Zattere ai Gesuati
Dorsoduro
Tel.528 68 58
Fax 522 23 40
A charming 15th-century house
offering antique-filled public rooms
and bedrooms, plus fine views
across to the inner island suburb of
Giudecca and the pretty canal.
Half-board only. 36 rooms.

San Cassiano   II-III
(Ca'Favretto) (3-star)
Calle della Rosa
Santa Croce
Tel. 524 17 68
Fax 72 10 33
An atmospheric 14th-century palace with smart old-fashioned bedrooms; the most popular are those
overlooking the Grand Canal, facing the Ca'd'Oro. Wheelchair access. 35 rooms.

GIUDECCA

Cipriani
(4-star de luxe)
Giudecca
Tel. 520 77 44
Fax 520 39 30
Arguably Venice's most luxurious
hotel, it's the only one (outside the
Lido) to boast a swimming pool.
Housed in a beautiful villa in a
garden setting, the rooms have
every facility. Sauna and tennis
are available. Water taxis shuttle
guests to and from San Marco.
Wheelchair access. 98 rooms.

THE LIDO

Byron Centrale
(3-star)
Via Bragadin
Tel. 526 00 52/526 02 91
Fax 526 92 41
The Lido is a small attractive hotel
set back from the main road and
surrounded by its own garden.
Wheelchair access. 36 rooms.

Des Bains
(4-star)
Lungomare Marconi
Tel. 526 59 21
Fax 526 01 13
Forever associated with Visconti's
Death in Venice (part-written and
filmed here), this grand Art Deco

hotel with a large garden, two tennis courts and a swimming pool is
full of old-world *Belle Epoque* atmosphere. 195 rooms.

Excelsior
(5-star de luxe)
Lungomare Marconi
Tel. 526 02 01
Fax 526 72 76
The Lido's only five-star hotel
was built in the 1900s and billed
as the most glamorous resort hotel
in the world. It is richly decorated
in a Moorish-Gothic style and offers seven tennis courts and a
swimming pool. 218 rooms.

Quattro Fontane
(4-star)
Via delle Quattro Fontane
Tel. 526 02 27
Fax 526 07 26
A hotel of unusual and charming
North European chalet-style con-
struction, set in its own garden
with tennis courts. 72 rooms.

Rigel
(3-star)
Via Enrico Dandolo
Tel. 526 88 10/526 88 11
Fax 276 00 77
This friendly, small hotel is set in
its own garden and situated close
to the Piazzale Santa Mara Elisa-
bette. 42 rooms.

73

Recommended Restaurants

Below is a selection of some of Venice's best restaurants in different price bands. You are advised to book ahead in high season (from spring to autumn, and at Carnival and during Christmas week) for lunch and dinner. For the most popular restaurants, we recommend that you book ahead all year round in order to get the best seats.

Note that nearly all restaurants close at least one day per week, and that many also close during part of late July and August and January and February.

To give you an idea of price for a three-course meal for one (*antipasti* or *primi piatti*; *secondi piatti*; vegetables or salad; dessert or cheese) including cover and service, but excluding wine, we have used the following symbols:

▊▊▊▊	above L. 75,000
▊▊▊	L.55-75,000
▊▊	L.40-55,000
▊	up to L.40,000

SAN MARCO, CASTELLO, CANNAREGIO

Aciugheta ▊▊
Campo Santi Filippo e Giacomo, 4357, Castello
Tel. 522 42 92
Closed Wednesday. Highly popular and typical *trattoria*, with a lively terrace giving onto the bustling square. Try one of the specialities of the house: *pennette all'acciughe* (pasta quills with anchovy). Good pizzas and *cicheti* (snacks), excellent wines.

Al Conte Pescaor ▊▊
Piscina San Zulian, 544 San Marco
Tel. 522 14 83
Closed Sunday. Attractive traditional rustic *trattoria* with terrace. Renowned for simple fish dishes.

Al Covo ▊▊▊
Campiello della Pescheria, 3968 Castello
Tel. 522 38 12
Closed Wednesday and Thursday. Probably the city's most fashionable restaurant, run by a Venetian husband and Texan wife team,

using only seasonal produce to create an innovative menu specializing in fish and seafood.

Al Giardinetto da Severino

Ruga Giuffa, 4928
Castello
Tel. 528 53 32
Closed Thursday. *Trattoria* boasting an attractive rustic garden with contemporary artworks adorning its bamboo-covered walls. Typical Venetian home cooking, popular with locals and tourists.

Al Graspo de Ua

Calle dei Bombaseri, 5093
San Marco
Tel. 522 36 47, fax 523 39 17
Closed Monday and Tuesday. A large, friendly, old-school Italian *ristorante* serving Venetian and Italian specialities; try the *pesce spada* (swordfish) *alla Livornese* or *pollo alla crema di nocciola* (chicken in hazelnut sauce).

Antico Martini

Campo San Fantin, 2010
San Marco
Tel. 522 41 21, fax 528 98 57
Closed Tuesday lunchtime. Serving excellent gourmet food using only the finest ingredients and incorporating Italian and international influences into an inventive

menu. Elegant 18th-century interiors, smart terrace.

Antico Pignolo

Calle Specchieri, 451
San Marco
Tel. 522 8123, fax 520 90 07
Closed Tuesday (excluding September and October). A traditional Venetian *ristorante* with stuccoed walls and exposed beams. The extensive menu consists of Venetian *haute cuisine*, with several fish and seafood specialities and *fondue bourguignonne*.

La Caravella

Calle Larga 22 Marzo, 2397
San Marco
Tel. 520 89 01, fax 520 7131
Closed Wednesday. Venice's most cosmopolitan menu, featuring an extensive, mouthwatering range of Italian, Venetian and European dishes, served in a comfortable old-world atmosphere. The *bigoli in salsa* and the *scampi allo champagne* are highly recommended.

La Colomba

Piscina di Frezzeria, 1665
San Marco
Tel. 522 11 75, fax 522 14 68
Closed Wednesday (except May-Jun and Sept-Oct). This charming secluded spot by the Fenice theatre has been an artists' meeting

place for over 50 years and its modern interior is covered in contemporary artworks. Attractive outdoor terrace. *Flambés* are the house speciality.

Corte Sconta ▯▯▯
Calle del Pestrin, 3886
Castello
Tel. 522 70 24
Closed Sunday and also Monday. Many locals claim that this rather ordinary looking backstreet *trattoria* serves Venice's finest gourmet fare. Superb *antipasti* and seafood, outstanding house wine.

Da Ivo ▯▯▯▯
Ramo dei Fuseri, 1809
San Marco
Tel. 520 58 89
Closed Sunday. Beautifully decorated, atmospheric, small dining room serving first-class Venetian and Tuscan cuisine; look out for various Florentine specials including chicken and T-bone steak.

Da Raffaele ▯▯-▯▯▯
Campo San Moisè, 2367
San Marco
Tel. 528 99 40
Closed Thursday. Splendid canalside terrace, ideal for summer dining, right next to a gondolier's mooring point. In winter dine in baronial medieval surroundings.

Relatively short and simple menu, changing seasonally.

Do Forni ▯▯▯▯
Calle Specchieri, 468
San Marco
Tel. 523 21 48, fax 528 81 32
Closed Thursday (except June and October) and late November-early December. Offering excellent, cuisine either in a traditional rustic dining room or 'aboard' the Orient Express. Specials include risottos, chicken breast *Do Forni* and several fish dishes.

Fiaschetteria Toscana ▯-▯▯▯
Salizzada San Giovanni
Grisostomo, 5719, Cannaregio
Tel. 528 52 81
Closed Tuesday. Very smart, formal *ristorante* with an attractive terrace for outdoor dining. Fish specialities include the tasty *anguilla sull'ara con l'alloro* (baked eel with laurel) and the *rombo al burro nero e capperi* (turbot with black butter and capers).

Latteria Veneziana ▯
Calle dei Fuseri
San Marco
Telephone bookings
not necessary
Open lunchtime only. Closed on Sunday. Pleasant, simple and airy

osteria-like establishment on two floors offering vegetarian snacks and full meals; try *crespelle alla zucca* (pumpkin pancakes) or *verdure con scamorza* (vegetables with mature mozzarella).

Noemi
Calle Fabbri, 912
San Marco
Tel. 522 52 38
Closed Sunday. A venerable city favourite since 1928, Noemi now has a long and innovative menu of Venetian-based dishes. Try the smoked goose breast or a savoury éclair or crêpe to start, then a house fish speciality.

Osteria Al Mascaron
Calle Lunga Santa Maria Formosa, 5225, Castello
Tel. 522 59 95
Closed Sunday. Bustling traditional *osteria* with a young arty atmosphere. The short, daily-changing menu often features grilled fish, and there's also a tempting array of *cicheti* (snacks).

Osteria Assassini
Rio Terra degli Assassini, 3695
San Marco
Tel. 528 79 86
Closed Sunday. Lively and atmospheric pub-like establishment with a short, daily-changing menu of full meals (try to get a table on Wednesday, which is Venetian specialities day). There is also a good drinks selection.

Rivetta
Ponte San Provolo
off Campo Santi Filippo e Giacomo, 4625, Castello
Tel. 528 73 02
Closed Monday. Friendly, bustling *trattoria* with the emphasis on fish and fish-pasta dishes. The house is also proud of its *tiramisù* – with good reason. Good *cicheti*.

Taverna La Fenice
Campo San Fantin, San Marco
Tel. 522 38 56
Closed Sunday and Monday afternoon. Elegant restaurant, with typical Venetian atmosphere. Situated near the Fenice Theatre, it is open late after performances. Serves a variety of Venetian and international cuisine.

Trattoria da Remigio
Salizzada dei Greci, 3416
Castello
Tel. 523 00 89
Closed on Monday evening and Tuesday. Simple indoor *trattoria* highly popular with local people. Try the *gnocchi* and any one of the many house fish specials.

77

Vesuvio

Rio Tera Farsetti, 1837
Cannaregio
Tel. 71 89 68
Closed Wednesday. Very popular *pizzeria* famed for its wood-oven pizzas, but also offering very reasonably priced fish.

SANTA CROCE, SAN POLO, DORSODURO

Agli Alboreti

Rio Terra Antonio Foscarini, 882/4, Dorsoduro
Tel. 523 00 58, fax 521 01 58
Open evenings only, closed on Wednesday. Traditional and creative Venetian cuisine of the highest quality is served in charming surroundings; try the *scampi con cognac* or the *coda di rospo* (monkfish) *alle erbe fini*.

Ai Gondolieri

Corte delle Mende
San Vio, 366, Dorsoduro
Tel. 528 63 96
Closed Tuesday. Stylish, modern monochrome dining room where meat and vegetables prepared in elegant *nouvelle cuisine* style (and portions) and presentation are the house favourites (no fish or seafood). Try the stuffed courgettes and the speciality of the day.

Ai Mercanti

Pescheria di Rialto, 1588
San Polo
Tel. 524 02 82
Closed Sunday. Its convenient location, a few steps away from the fish market, ensures the best of the day's catch. Choose from several rooms, ranging in character, as well as from several varied and inventive set menus.

Alla Madonna

Calle della Madonna, 594
San Polo
Tel. 522 38 24
Closed on Wednesday. Venice's most famous medium-price fish restaurant is a bustling warren of beamed and stuccoed rooms, catering for a variety of tastes – tourists, locals, students and business people alike congregate here.

Alla Zucca

Ponte del Megio
off Campo San Giacomo
dell'Orio, 1762, Santa Croce
Tel. 524 15 70
Closed Sunday. This small, modern café is characterized by its pleasant and relaxed atmosphere. Pavement tables provide outdoor dining and a good vantage point. There is a daily changing menu, strong on pasta and vegetable dishes; and good desserts too.

Al Nono Risorto

*Sottoportego de Siora Bettina, off
Campo San Cassiano, 2337
Sant Croce
Tel. 524 11 69*
Closed Wednesday and Thursday
morning. Authentic, no-frills *trat-
toria/pizzeria* with a pretty shaded
garden. Short menu changes daily.

Antica Trattoria
Poste Vecchie

*Pescheria, San Polo, 1608
Tel. 72 18 22*
Closed Tuesday. One of the city's
oldest and most attractive restaurants, comprising a warren of tiny,
atmospheric, traditionally decorated rooms, some dating back to the
16th century. Fish predominates.

Antico Capon

*Campo Santa Margherita, 3004
Dorsoduro
Tel. 528 52 52*
Closed Wednesday. Busy, unaf-
fected *trattoria/pizzeria* with tables
on the popular square of Santa
Margherita. Simple menu, plus a
choice of 46 wood-oven pizzas.

Caffè Orientale

*Calle del Caffettier, 2426
San Polo
Tel. 71 98 04, fax 71 51 67*
Closed Sunday evening and Mon-
day. Dine in the stylish modern

dining room in winter and on the
canal-side terrace in summer. Typical Venetian food with the emphasis on fish – try *bacalà veneziana,
orata, triglia* (red mullet).

Da Fiore

*Calle del Scaleter, 3461
San Polo
Tel. 523 53 10*
Closed Sunday, Monday. Simplicity and food of the highest quality
are the key ingredients to the success of this highly rated establishment. Short, changing menu, very
strong on seafood, served in a
cool, classy, marble dining room.

Locanda Montin

*Fondamente di Borgo, 1147
San Trovaso, Dorsoduro
Tel. 522 71 51, fax 520 02 55*
Closed on Tuesday evening and
Wednesday. The food may draw
mixed reviews but the setting, a
stunning garden shaded by huge
pergolas, is unforgettable. Try the
granceola, filetto di bue branzino
(steak) or the *grigliata dell'Adriatico* (mixed grill).

Pizzeria Al Profeta

*Calle Lunga de Santa Barbara,
2671, Dorsoduro
Tel. 523 74 66*
Closed Monday. Friendly *tratto-
ria-cum-pizzeria* with a pleasant **79**

outdoor terrace and an extensive menu – over 60 pizzas and several fish specialities including *gnochetti al pesce*, *spaghetti al caparozzoli* and *seppie* (cuttlefish) *nere*.

Taverna San Trovaso

Fondamente Priuli, 1016
Dorsoduro
Tel. 520 37 03
Closed Monday. Popular, friendly *pizzeria/trattoria*, often full of locals and families. Book a table downstairs in the brick-vaulted room. Good value *menù turistico*.

Trattoria San Tomà

Campo San Tomà, 2864/2
San Polo
Tel. 523 88 19
Closed Tuesday. Fine location with tables on a charming square and a rear garden. This trattoria is known for its excellent pizzas but also specializes in *pasta all'uovo* and *magret de canard*. Look out too for *baudroie* (devil-fish).

Terrazza Sommariva

Riva del Vin, San Polo, 371
Tel. 523 18 47
Closed Tuesday. One of several restaurants lining the bank by the Rialto, with a romantic view of the famous bridge. Try the pasta in mushroom sauce and the *fegato* (liver) *veneziana*.

THE ISLANDS

Ai Frati

Fondamente Venier, 4
Murano
Tel. 73 66 94
Closed Thursday. This is Murano's best fish and seafood restaurant, and very popular, too. For a pleasant, relaxing dining experience, choose a table outdoors on a mooring platform on the island's very own Canal Grande. (You can also dine indoors.)

Ai Pescatori

Via Galuppi, 371
Burano
Tel. 73 06 50, fax 73 06 61
Closed Wednesday. The perfect place to get acquainted with Burano seafood. This aptly named restaurant on the island's main street is a proudly owned family establishment that lives up to its reputation. Try *petits crabes en friture, anguilla à la sauce de Burano*.

Al Trono di Attila

Fondamente Borgogni, 7
Torcello
Tel. 73 00 94
Closed Monday. The menu is standard Venetian fare but the beautiful garden setting, close to the Ponte del Diavolo, is simply idyllic. Good value for money.

As for the **Palazzo Mocenigo** complex (Gothic to 18th century), marked by the blue-and-white mooring posts (*pali*), it was the home of Lord Byron for two years. He started writing *Don Juan* here in 1818. His most daring Venetian achievement, however, was to swim in a race against two other men from the Lido all the way to the Rialto. An excellent swimmer, he was the only one to finish. Today, the Grand Canal is no longer clean enough for such aquatic feats.

You are unlikely to miss the banners draped from the **Palazzo Grassi**, announcing its latest important exhibition. This fine mid-18th-century palace now serves as a cultural centre.

The graceful, almost Japanese-style **Accademia Bridge** was built as a temporary wooden arch in 1932, replacing an iron structure which had become an obstruction to larger *vaporetti*. It has been here ever since and is a favourite lookout point with a picture-postcard view of the Salute. The splendid building to the left, with the classic red-and-white *pali*, is the 15th-century **Cavalli Franchetti** palace. Adjacent is the Grand Canal side of the **Palazzi Barbaro** (15th-17th century), much favoured by the artistic and literary set, where artists Robert Browning, Henry James, John Singer Sargent, Claude Monet and James Whistler all spent some time.

THE RIGHT BANK

The **Fondaco dei Turchi**, built in the 13th century, is one of the Grand Canal's oldest survivors and, although heavily restored, it is a typical example of its day. Once the Turkish warehouse, it now houses Venice's Natural History Museum (see p.62).

The **Palazzo** or **Ca'Pésaro**, completed in 1682, is an immense and impressive Baroque building, decorated with grotesque masks (see p.62).

The **Rialto market buildings** include the Fabbriche Nuove, a Sansovino project of 1554, now a law court, and the Fabbriche Vecchie (*c*.1520). The building housing the fish market (*pescheria*) is of more **81** modern construction; it dates from 1907. If the tracery of the mid-13th-century **Palazzo Bernardo** looks familiar, that's because it has been copied from the Doges' Palace; nevertheless, this is one of the Canal's most splendid buildings.

On the bend of the canal (known as the *volta*), look out for an attractive trio of palaces, first the **Balbi** (1590), then the **Ca'Fóscari** (1437), currently home to the University, and finally the **Giustinian** (*c*.1452), where Wagner composed part of *Tristan und Isolde*. Three blocks along is the glorious 17th-century **Ca'Rezzonico**.

Although architecturally inferior, the **Palazzo Barbarigo** has some colourful, late-19th-century mosaics. Close by, the **Palazzo Venier dei Leoni** is an intriguing landmark on the canal. Now home to the excellent Guggenheim Collection (see p.51), the building was never finished, and its first and only storey features an attractive and unusual platform jutting into the water.

One of the most charming and picturesque of all Venetian palaces on the Grand Canal is the comparatively small **Dario** (1487), which has a beautiful, subtly coloured marble façade and typically Venetian chimney pots, funnel-shaped to catch sparks and therefore reduce the risk of fires.

GONDOLAS AND GONDOLIERS

Nothing is more quintessentially Venetian than the gondola. It has been around, in one form or another, since the 11th century and, at its peak in the 18th century, the city counted at least 14,000 of this unique craft. Today, though far from being extinct, the canals count less than 500 gondolas.

Gondolas are a very uniform species: 10.87m (around 36ft) in length, with a maximum width of 1.42m (around 4ft) and a maximum height of 0.64m (2ft) at the centre. Curiously, the boat is asymmetrical (the left side is 24cm/9in wider than the right) in order to assist the equally asymmetrical position taken up by the gondolier to row and steer.

All gondolas are painted black, in deference still to the sumptuary laws of 1562, which attempted to curb the extravagances of boat owners (and of Venetian society in general). However, they do retain little brass 'sea-horses' amidships and the rather curious metallic pronged prow (or *ferro*).

Several unconvincing explanations have been offered for the symbolism and the shape of the *ferro*; according to one school of thought, the blades represent the six *sestieri*, while others maintain that the shape

Art and watercrafts. Did any city ever possess such a graceful means of transport?

suggests the Grand Canal or even possibly the doge's cap.

Each gondola is constructed by hand from approximately 280 separate pieces of wood, namely fir, larch, cherry, elm, mahogany, lime, oak and walnut, Look in at the Squero di San Trovaso (see p.54), and you may be lucky enough to see one being made.

Gondola travel today is almost exclusively restricted to tourists. Although not cheap, it need not be expensive if you share the cost of the trip (five is the boat's maximum capacity). And, for a handful of small change, anyone can cross the Grand Canal by *traghetto*, the two-man gondola ferry service. It is customary, though not obligatory, to stand during the crossing.

Many gondoliers still wear the traditional outfit of straw boater, striped tee-shirt and white sailor top, though these days they never sing. A crooner has to be ordered separately and is most often heard accompanying a mini-flotilla of gondolas winding their way through the backwaters.

Cannaregio

GHETTO

For almost 300 years, until Napoleon ended the abhorrent practice in 1797, the Jews of Venice were forced to live in this tiny section of Cannaregio, surrounded on all sides by canals. The *sestiere* name of Ghetto subsequently came to denote Jewish, then deprived quarters all over the world.

Jewish refugees fleeing the War of Cambrai in 1508 came in their thousands to settle here. At their peak, in the 17th century, they numbered some 5,000 – the limit-ed space produced tenements six storeys high that still rank among Venice's tallest buildings. They were severely taxed, all forced to wear distinctive clothing, barred from many professions and forced to observe a curfew, which was strictly enforced by gates and watchmen. Yet, in an increasingly hostile world, here at least Jews were tolerated.

Not much remains of those harsh days, though this is still

one of Venice's poorest areas. The Jewish community in the district has diminished to only 30 members, and another 600 populate the rest of the city. The **Museo Ebraico** (Jewish Museum) gives a fascinating insight into their history and offers guided tours of synagogues dating back to the 16th century. The museum is closed on Saturday.

On the opposite side of the square to the museum, a poignant series of reliefs commemorates the 202 Venetian Jews deported to Nazi death camps in 1943 and 1944.

CA'D'ORO

This 15th-century palace on the Grand Canal is more famous for its façade than its contents, but it is well worth the detour across the water to look at the Italian art on display inside. Note that the building is closed on Monday.

The Gothic interiors have largely been stripped to make way for modern gallery space. The principal exhibit is Mantegna's striking *St Sebastian*,

one of the city's most memorable and painful images. Here you can also see minor works by Tintoretto and Titian and a series of frescos recovered from other buildings.

Elsewhere, more fine paintings and some delightful Venetian sculptures, bronzes and reliefs make this a good collection on a modest scale.

Secluded villas on the canals are typical of Venice's supremely elegant architecture.

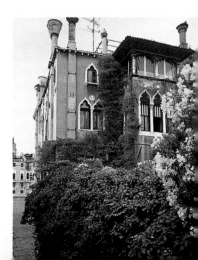

Sacred Venice

If you have more than a few days to spend in Venice, or if you are already familiar with the city's better-known landmarks, you may like to seek out some of the following Venetian churches.

SANTI GIOVANNI E PAOLO (SAN ZANIPOLO)

San Zanipolo (the Venetian habit of slurring names together is perfectly illustrated in the dialect name) is one of the two largest churches in Venice after San Marco, disputing second place with its great Gothic sister, the Frari (see p.59). It was completed in 1430 for the Dominican order. It is known today as Venice's Pantheon, since so many doges (25 in all) and republican dignitaries lie within. Like the Frari, the church is cavernous, with graphic sculptures adorning its tombs – look in the south aisle for the tomb of Marcantonio Bragadin, the commander flayed alive by **86** the Turks in Famagusta in 1571.

Two of the church's most memorable art treasures to look out for are Giovanni Bellini's early polyptych (in the right-hand nave) and Lorenzo Lotto's mellow-toned St Antonine (in the south transept).

In the *campo* outside the church is a superb 15th-century equestrian statue by Andrea Verrochio and Alessandro Leopardi. The rider is a Venetian general, Bartolomeo Colleoni, who left a large legacy to the city on condition that a statue of him was raised next to the Basilica di San Marco. The city took the money but ignored the condition attached to it – after all, not even doges were accorded that honour. As a compromise, the statue was erected eventually in front of the Scuola di San Marco – the tenuous San Marco association presumably saved the municipal conscience.

The splendid façade of the **Scuola di San Marco** dates from the late 15th century and is notable for its curious *trompe l'œil* panels on the lower section. Its walls now house the civic hospital.

A myriad red-tiled roofs dot the Venetian skyline. In the background, the bulk of the Santi Giovanni e Paolo looms large.

SANTA MARIA DEI MIRACOLI

Close to San Zanipolo in the north of the Castello district lies one of the city's favourite and most delightful churches. Venetians call it their *scrigno d'oro* (or golden jewel box) and they like to get married here.

Those pioneers and patrons of early Renaissance architecture, the great Lombardo fami-ly, built this surprisingly small church in eight years (1481-1489), marbling the inner and outer walls and covering its arched ceiling with portraits of holy men. The result is a very charming church, secreted behind the Rialto Bridge amidst a warren of canals and houses, though unfortunately there is no current access to the interior due to restoration.

87

MADONNA DELL'ORTO

The 15th-century church of our Lady of the Garden occupies a quiet spot in Cannaregio. This is Tintoretto's church. It was the great Renaissance painter's parish place of worship and he is buried with his family to the right of the choir, near the high altar. Not surprisingly, the Madonna dell'Orto also contains two of his finest paintings. Soaring 164m (50ft) up each side of the high altar are his *Last Judgement* and *The Worship of the Golden Calf.* Several more of Tintoretto's works adorn the interior, of which the dramatic *Presentation of the Virgin* (over the sacristy door) is also greatly admired.

Look out too for Cima da Conegliano's remarkable painting of *St John the Baptist* to the right of the entrance.

The church, with its striking Gothic façade and delightful cloister, was built to house a miraculous statue of the Virgin and Child, found in a nearby garden (*orto*). Strategically located just across the canal in front of the church is a leading Venetian undertaker; black funeral boats trimmed with gold lions are frequently to be seen moored outside.

SAN NICOLÒ DEI MENDICOLI

Set behind the docks, this humble parish church in a poor area of Dorsoduro is often overlooked. Built between the 12th and 15th centuries, it intriguingly combines rich decoration with a modest exterior. Restored by the Venice in Peril Fund in 1977 (see p.32), its beautiful madonnas and gilt arches are resplendent in the entrancing candle-lit interior.

SAN SEBASTIANO

Not far from San Nicolò dei Mendicoli, near the docks in Dorsoduro, this splendid 16th-century church is a glittering tribute to Paolo Veronese, who painted most of the colourful, sensuous works decorating the walls, altar and fantastic ceiling. The artist is also buried here, but the church is closed for major renovation.

The Islands

A highlight of any visit to Venice is, of course, venturing out on a *vaporetto* into that inviting lagoon. Many of its small islands are simply uninhabited wilderness, and inaccessible by public transport. But no visitor with more than a few days to spare should miss the serenity of Torcello or the vivid colours of Burano. Here are some suggestions for leisurely half-day or one-day island excursions.

SAN GIORGIO MAGGIORE

This is the nearest island, within swimming distance of the Doges' Palace, and it forms the

*V*iew from the Campanile of San Giorgio Maggiore, down into the monastery and the Canale della Giudecca.

backdrop to countless photographs, looking back towards Venice. As swimming is not recommended, take the No. 52 *vaporetto*. The short journey to Palladio's splendid **church** and monastery of San Giorgio Maggiore lasts no more than five minutes.

The church took 45 years from design (1565) to completion (1610), but the result is a masterpiece of proportion and harmonious space. Tintoretto's *Last Supper* and *The Shower of Manna* (both 1592-94) grace either side of the chancel. The high altar, meanwhile, is dominated by a large bronze group by Girolamo Campagna, representing the Evangelists sustaining the world, a work that took two years to create (1591-93). Behind are some splendidly carved choirstalls, dating from the same period.

For most visitors, however, the church takes second place to the **view** from its 200-year-old campanile. Take the lift to the top for one of the finest panoramas of Venice, then look down into the cloister of the monastery below to see a rare grassy space. Officially there is no entry to the monastery other than by prior arrangement (tel. 528 99 00). If the gate (adjacent to the church) is left ajar, you may be able to peep inside or, if your Italian is sufficient to charm the gatekeeper, you may be allowed to walk round the cloister.

SAN MICHELE

San Michele, the 'Island of the Dead' is Venice's famous cemetery island, lying 400m (440yd) from Fondamente Nuove. (A Napoleonian decree set forth its installation.) The No. 52 *vaporetto* stops right outside the church of San Michele, an elegant building but lacking any outstanding artistic feature.

Go through the cloister to reach the cemetery – it's open to visitors daily from 7.30am until 4pm. Here among the cypress trees, look out for the graves of American poet Ezra Pound (1885-1972) in section XV, and the Russian composer Igor Stravinsky (1882-1971) and impresario Serge Diaghilev (1872-1929) in section XIV.

MURANO

After San Michele, the No. 52 *vaporetto* stops at Murano, the little island of the glass blowers. Many visitors arrive here by *motoscafi*, organized by individual glass factories whose representatives accost visitors around the Piazza with importunate enthusiasm. The offer of a free ride is also likely to be made through your hotel. If you prefer not to be subjected to high-pressure sales tactics once you're on the island, take the *vaporetto* and make your own way around the factories.

Glass was manufactured in Venice as far back as the 10th century, but the open furnaces presented such a fire hazard that, around 1292, the doge ordered the factories to be transferred to Murano.

Grouped here together, the glass blowers kept the secrets of their trade for centuries; the manufacture of mirrors, for instance, was for a long time exclusive to Venice. The Muranese may have invented the first spectacles (around the beginning of the 14th century) and they certainly made the largest and clearest window panes in the whole of Europe.

The island prospered; by the early 16th century its population reached 30,000. Glass artisans were honoured citizens and accorded extra privileges.

Rest in Peace?

Nowhere is Venice's chronic lack of available land brought home so vividly as on the cemetery island of San Michele. It was Napoleon who decreed that burials should no longer take place in the city, and on San Michele they are not so much welcomed as tolerated for ten years. Unless the deceased has made provision for an extension on his or her final lease (and few Venetians can afford it), then at the end of that time the remains are exhumed and sent to an ossuary to make way for the next occupant!

Murano's crystalware decorated royal palaces abroad and its sumptuous villas housed the leading nobles and diplomats of the city.

But, as other countries learned and applied the secrets of Murano, so the island's importance declined. By the 19th century, most of its grand old summer residences had gone. However, the trade was revived in the 19th century and continues today, though not up to its old standards. Unfortunately, the decline in quality has been matched by an unjustifiable increase in price.

For an interesting perspective on the history of Venetian glass, visit the **Museo Vetrario** (Glass Museum), housed in a truly delightful 17th-century bishop's palace. There's also a modern adjunct, the **Modern & Contemporary Glass Museum** on Fondamenta Manin. Note that both museums are closed on Wednesday.

Orientation in Murano is a simple matter. After the main quay, where you disembark at the Colonna *vaporetto* stop, stroll along the picturesque Fondamenta dei Vetrai, which leads to Murano's very own Grand Canal.

Cross the bridge to the other side and follow the canal to the right, until you get to the Glass Museum and the **Church of Santi Maria e Donato**. Some say this is the oldest church in Venice, and its foundations may pre-date San Marco, going back to the 7th century. Whatever the truth of this claim, the church is splendidly atmospheric, and both the brightly coloured 12th-century mosaic floor and a golden mosaic of the Madonna over the high altar have been restored with great care and sympathy.

In a city where dragons are almost as much an obsession as lions, it is interesting to note the giant bones behind the altar. They are said to be those of a dragon slain by St Donato. Unlike St George, Donato eschewed the conventional lance

This delicate figure is representative of the still much sought-after Murano glass.

and sword; he slew the beast simply by spitting at it!

BURANO

You can continue on the No. 12 *vaporetto* from Murano to Burano, but the service runs only every hour. Another option is to catch the No. 14 from San Zaccaria. The journey to Burano and the neighbouring

island of Torcello takes around 45 minutes.

Burano is often described as the 'pearl of the lagoon', and it is undoubtedly a real gem. Imagine a section of Venice, scaled down, with tiny houses and canals, and then washed in glorious pastel shades. The bright buildings in a rainbow of blues, reds, peppermint, russet and yellow are a refreshing contrast to the grey walls of the mainland.

The island once produced the world's finest lace and its famous *punto in aria* pattern was the most sought after in Europe. Today, this fine art is dying, principally because the high price of the finished product does compare unfavourably with imported substitutes, but also because young Buranese girls prefer to pursue less painstaking careers.

The only place you will see Buranese lacemakers today is in the **Scuola dei Merletti** (on the opposite side of the main square to the church).

The school opened in 1872 to retrain the island's women at a time when the numbers of **93** skilled lacemakers had dwindled to just one. There is a small museum attached.

Before leaving the square, visit the 16th-century church, famous for its landmark leaning campanile (18th century). San Martino also houses the island's only art treasure, Giambattista Tiepolo's *Calvary*.

The main street of Via Baldessare Galuppi is well served with fish restaurants, reflecting the male side of the island's economy. Fishing boats dot the shores of Burano and some are

moored right outside the houses – a most colourful and picturesque sight.

You won't need a map in Burano. Although larger than Murano, it is a delightful place to wander at will, and you're unlikely to get lost if you use the church campanile as your reference point.

From Burano, the peaceful island of **San Francesco del Deserto** makes a charming detour. The trip takes about 20 minutes and can be arranged with the boatman on the main square of Burano. St Francis is said to have landed on the island in 1220 and Franciscan friars have been here almost ever since. A handful of the brethren choose to make this a permanent home, while young novices spend a year here as part of their training. The monastery, which has a beautiful 14th-century cloister and gardens, is open to visitors from around 9 until 11am and from 3 to 5.30pm.

TORCELLO

'Mother and Daughter, you behold them both in their widowhood' wrote John Ruskin of

The rainbow houses of Burano are a real eye-opener after the muted brickwork of the mainland. **95**

Taking in the sun – these curious antiquities decorate a wall at Torcello.

Torcello's relationship to Venice. Whether shrewd observation or fanciful nonsense, it is impossible not to reflect on this line as you note the beautiful Mother and Child relief high on a wall, just after you step off the boat.

Amazing as it seems now, this overgrown, almost deserted island was up until early medieval times the lagoon's principal civilization, with an estimated population of 20,000.

But with the silting up of its canals into marshes, a consequent outbreak of malaria, and the ascendancy of Venice, there was a mass exodus from the island. Today there are about one hundred people here, though it seems much less.

As you walk from the *vaporetto* stage to the cathedral, the canal is the only familiarly Venetian feature. On Torcello, tall buildings have given way to trees, fields and thick undergrowth, and the urban hum is replaced by soft birdsong and leaves rustling in the breeze.

The solitary path leads past an ancient **bridge** without a parapet (*Ponte del Diavolo*, or Bridge of the Devil), a handful of attractive restaurants and some itinerant lace-sellers, to a small square which houses Torcello's cathedral, the Church of Santa Fosca and the Museo dell'Estuario (or Museum of the Estuary).

Santa Fosca was built during the 11th and 12th centuries and has a bare simplicity rarely found in Venetian churches. Somewhat over-restored, it is still a place of great serenity.

The **Museo dell'Estuario** houses a small but interesting collection of pieces from local, long disappeared churches and other architectural fragments. Outside the museum, note the primitive stone chair, known as 'Attila's throne'. It is possibly an early judge's seat.

Torcello's present Cathedral of **Santa Maria dell'Assunta** dates mostly from 1008. It is a beautiful, spacious building, also with a very peaceful atmosphere. The high altar dates from the 7th century and here you can see the body of Saint Heliodorus, the first Bishop of Altinum (whence the island's first settlers originally came), complete with gold mask. The Roman sarcophagus close by was his original tomb.

The church's principal attractions are its **mosaics**. The blue and gold stones of the tearful *Virgin and Child* and the *Apostles* in the apse are Byzantine masterpieces as old as the church. At the opposite end, an entire wall is covered by an equally impressive and ancient (though much restored) *Last Judgement*. Experts maintain that these are the finest mosaics in Italy outside Ravenna.

LIDO

Although the *Belle Epoque* atmosphere of this barrier island has long since disappeared, the name Lido still conjures up images of cosmopolitan glamour: the place where the 'beautiful people' tan on the beach by day, and flutter with their fortunes by night in the summer casino.

If you want to sit on the beach alongside them, you will have to pay an extremely high admission price, as much of the Lido's 10km-long beach strip has been appropriated and sectioned off by private owners, hotels and municipal establishments. Alternatively, you could try the public beaches, but these are of poorer quality and, free or paid for, the water is subject to pollution.

Today's characterless island of long, straight roads is a far cry from the days of the doges, when noble Venetians hunted in the Lido's woods and grassy wastes. More recently, Lord **97**

On the beach... The Lido, evocative of the Bèlle Epoque's cosmopolitan glamour, still throngs with people in high season.

Byron loved to walk and ride here. Now the grassy wastes have been turned into manicured golf courses and few people walk anywhere. Driving is permitted on the Lido, though there is a reasonable bus service which will get you to most parts of the island.

Aside from its beach and various sporting opportunities, the Lido is also the scene of the 'Marriage to the Sea' ceremony on Ascension Day, and plays host once a year to the International Film Festival during the late summer.

In high season the strip is boisterously alive with tourists, but after October, the crowds disappear and the Lido takes on a rather ghostly appearance.

What to Do

Shopping

Venice offers a dazzling concentration of shops with enticing window displays. A highly fashion-conscious city, its quality items rival those of Florence or Paris for elegance and style. However, high style invariably comes with a high price tag, and you are unlikely to find any real bargains. Inevitably, there's also a great amount of tawdry junk.

The most expensive shops are to be found around Piazza San Marco. Here too are clustered the plastic gondola and tacky souvenir T-shirt vendors. However, some very attractive art as well as pretty costume and ethnic jewellery is sold around the Piazza and on the Riva degli Schiavoni.

The main shopping street is the Merceria, which runs from beneath the Torre dell'Orologio to the Rialto. The quality of retail outlets varies, but the prices here are competitive.

It's worth browsing around the Rialto or along the Strada Nuova, which leads to the railway station, for more economical purchases. As with most things in Venice, you'll often find the best little shops in the most unlikely quarters. Look around the University area for arts and crafts, or the Rialto for foodstuffs. A delightful aspect of Venice's shops is their intimacy; the concept of department stores has yet to catch on here.

Art, Antiques: rarely will you see so much painting, drawing, sculpture, pottery and handicrafts for sale in one place as in Venice. Art galleries and antique shops abound, but prices are well above the average tourist's holiday budget. However, quay- and canal-side artists are often the source of good quality pictures, and in museums and galleries you can buy exquisite art posters. Look out for beautiful hand-printed and marbled papers, reflecting an old Venetian craft tradition. Antique or flea markets take place at Campo San Maurizio; enquire at the tourist office.

Glass and Lace: Murano is the place with the widest choice of glassware, but its prices are not necessarily the best. All high quality Venetian crystal is expensive and, of course, highly breakable, so you should insist on sturdy packaging if you do find something you want to buy. Bear in mind, too, that standards of craftsmanship are not as good as they once were, so be circumspect in your purchases. Real Burano lace is probably best bought on Burano, but make sure you're not offered a cheaper foreign import instead of the genuine article. Do your homework first in the lace museum.

Leather: accessories are usually the most affordable items. You won't find many bargains, but you can be assured of that renowned Italian sense of style.

Masks: a few traditional artisans around town still make wonderfully theatrical masks of papier-mâché (*cartapesta*). Possibly Venice's most distinctive souvenir, they owe their **100** popularity to the revival of Carnival (see p.105). Masks are both benign and sinister, and available in an amazing range of shapes, sizes and colours.

Entertainment

Nightlife

With an elderly resident population and a large number of day-only trippers, nightlife is, unsurprisingly, somewhat restrained. A relaxing place to make for after your evening meal is the **Piazza**, where you can simply order an espresso, listen to the bands and generally soak up the enchanting Venetian atmosphere.

Away from the Piazza, there is a scattering of late-night bars, mostly frequented by students and trendy young Venetians. You'll find these nightspots listed in the free leaflet *Notturno Veneziano*, which is sometimes available from the tourist information office. The booklet produced by Rolling Venice (see p.131) gives similar information. Venice has one **disco**, the Club El Souk in Dorsoduro (close to the Accademia), and there's also one on the Lido, the Acropolis. Both tend to be spurned by the locals, however, and if you want to be at the centre of the action, there's no better place than the lively student **bars** and **cafés** of Dorsoduro, particularly those around Campo Santa Margherita.

The smart hotels often have **piano-bar** lounges catering for older age groups, although there is no dancing. The most renowned is the Martini Scala in Campo San Fantin.

Venice's **casino**, a municipal institution, holds forth at the Lido in spring and summer and moves to the Palazzo Vendramin Calergi on the Grand Canal for the rest of the year. You can play roulette, chemin de fer, baccarat and black jack (21) until well into the morning. Don't forget to take your

Making faces; Venetian masks vary from high quality art to cheap souvenirs.

passport in order to gain admittance to the gambling rooms. Men must also wear a jacket and tie. The summer casino at the Lido also stages a regular programme of various pop concerts and discos.

The Arts

Despite the city's quiet nocturnal life, Venice offers an excellent full year-round schedule of classical music, dance, cinema, theatre and art exhibitions. In odd-numbered years, the famous Biennale of Contemporary Arts is staged between June and September.

Venice's churches frequently stage **musical events** ranging from a simple organ recital to choral concerts. Venues include Santo Stefano, the Frari and 'Vivaldi's Church' on the Riva degli Schiavoni. For details of programmes, consult Venice's comprehensive listings magazine, *Un Ospite di Venezia*, or simply keep an eye open for colourful fly posters advertising current attractions.

La Fenice (The Phoenix) has been called Europe's prettiest **theatre**, and it is certainly one of the oldest. In its gilded interior, this glittering gem stages opera, symphonic and choral concerts, ballet and modern dance, except in August when the theatre is closed. The other theatre of note is the Teatro Goldoni, also situated in the San Marco district, which of-

*B*iennale Man! The cutting edge of contemporary art, or art for art's sake?

Biennale

The *Biennale* is one of the oldest and most important exhibitions of contemporary art in the world. It began in 1895, rather incongruously as a royal silver wedding anniversary celebration and has been celebrated regularly ever since. Until recently it was held in even-numbered years, but it has now reverted to odd numbers and is staged between June and September.

The exhibition takes place mostly in some 40 pavilions of the Biennale Gardens, but a few events also take place in various centrally located venues. Each pavilion is sponsored by a different country and shows some avant-garde aspect of their art, often combined with wry political comment.

fers a fine programme of plays all year round.

Opera fans may like to note the summer programme at the Arena di Verona. **Rock** bands also call at this musical venue and at nearby Padua.

From late August until early September, the renowned Venice Film Festival attracts **cinema** specialists and celebrities as well as the usual hopefuls to the Lido. It's difficult, almost impossible, for ordinary tourists to see the films, however, although there are several cinema screens throughout the city – but no permanent foreign-language cinema.

Festivals

Venice has relatively few major set-piece events in the year. The culmination of the **Festa del Redentore** in July is a pyrotechnics display worth planning your trip around; the **Film Festival** is second only in terms of prestige to Cannes; the **Regata Storica** in September is the day the Grand Canal turns the clock back to the colours and finery of Venice's golden age, while the pageant of **La Sensa** (Ascension Day) is when Venice's 'Marriage to the Sea' is commemorated.

This bizarre ritual evolved from the grand celebrations **103**

Calendar of Events

For the most up-to-date information on the city's festivals' and arts' calendar, consult the tourist information office and local listings and press. The following review gives a taste of some of the major events.

Carnevale	*10 days before Lent*	Founded 1094, revived 1979; music, comedy, drama and a proliferation of costume masks.
La Sensa	*Sunday after Ascension*	Historic feast, taken from Ascension Day.
Festa del Redentore	*Third Sunday in July*	Commemorating the end of the plague in 1576; most celebrations take place the preceding Saturday night, with picnics and a fire works' display on the lagoon.
Venice Film Festival	*Early September*	Second only to Cannes; tickets for films are available on the day of performance.
Regata Storica	*First Sunday in September*	Renaissance-costume pageant and boat races on the Grand Canal.
Festa della Salute	*21 November*	This festival celebrates the end of the 1631 plague with a bridge of boats across the Grand Canal to Santa Maria della Salute.

following Venice's first ever successful sea campaign. (It was waged by Doge Pietro Orseolo II against Dalmatian pirates around 1000.) These celebrations reached their peak in 1177 when, in thanks for the Venetians' subjugation of Emperor Barbarossa, Pope Alexander III gave the doge a gold ring to wed Venice to the sea. Thereafter, each year on Ascension Day, the doge would board his fabulous *Bucintoro* and was rowed out to the Lido. Here he threw a gold ring into the sea as a symbol of the marriage and this initiated a series of celebrations.

Today's festivities, only recently revived, are rather more muted. The Mayor re-enacts the part of the doge and flings a ring into the waters, but there are few revelries afterwards. There is, however, the **Vogalonga** ('long row') to watch – a rowing regatta open to any oared boat which can cover the 32km (20 miles) from San Marco to Burano and back. As many as 1,500 boats take part with the fastest covering the course in around 90 minutes.

Carnevale

It's impossible to be unaware of Carnival's significance at any time of year – mask decorations, mask shops, posters, calendars and the occasional street theatre are all there to remind you of this festival.

Like other Carnival festivities throughout the world, the celebrations represent the last opportunity for feasting before the abstinence of Lent. What gives Venice's Carnival its special atmosphere, however, are the masks and costumes worn during this time.

The black cloak, the tricorn hat, the white mask and the rest of the rather sinister-looking garb mostly date back to the *commedia dell'arte* characters of the 18th century. Astonishingly perhaps, Venetians once wore these costumes for six months of each year, guaranteeing them virtual anonymity – while also enabling them to commit all sorts of misdemeanours in a prolonged carnival of fun and debauchery in which the class system was temporarily suspended.

105

Today's celebrations are rather more restrained, and compared to Carnival in other parts of the world, Venice's is still relatively tame. Nonetheless, this is one time of year that the city really comes to life with street parties, masked balls, pageants and special events, details of which can be obtained at the tourist office.

Sports

Venice itself offers virtually no leisure facilities for the sports-inclined visitor, but if you feel the need for exercise after a surfeit of culture (or pasta), there is a stadium on the Isola de Sant'Elena at the eastern tip of the city. Otherwise, the Lido is the place to go to satisfy your requirements.

Most of the private beaches of the large hotels offer a variety of **watersports**, including windsurfing, water-skiing, canoeing, dinghy and catamaran sailing. Less energetic pursuits include pedaloes or being towed along on the 'water banana'. These only operate dur-

ing the relatively short summer season (June to September).

The Venetians may take to the water like ducks but there's little chance of tourists hiring a boat on the lagoon. This is because too many visitors in the past have piloted boats irresponsibly and have tested the rescue service beyond reasonable limits. The lagoon may look like a big open pond, but below the surface is a maze of silted channels, just waiting to catch the unwary keel on its sandy banks.

You may be able to hire a motor launch and driver but the cost is prohibitively expensive. However, if you belong to a rowing club at home and can produce evidence of membership, then one of the local rowing clubs may well let you join their ranks temporarily. It's always best to write in advance; try the Società Cannottieri Bucintoro, Zattere, 15, Venice.

Budding gondoliers might also like to note that this particular club gives a rather unusual form of training: namely for rowing your craft while in the standing position.

Regatta preparations on the Zattere. Most Venetians take their boating very seriously.

Swimming from the beaches of the Lido can never be wholeheartedly recommended due to pollution from the mainland and the build-up of algae, which varies from year to year. However, some of the more exclusive hotels do have their own swimming pools (the only public swimming pool in Venice belongs to the luxurious Hotel Cipriani, which charges non-residents an expensive admission fee).

Aside from watersports, an 18-hole **golf** course on the Lido is open all year round with clubs for hire. There are four **tennis** clubs on the island, all open to the public; and **horse-riding** stables operate from Ca'Bianca.

The Lido tourist information office should be able to provide you with more details.

107

Children's Venice

Although Venetian art and architecture are not likely to appeal to most children, with a little imagination and planning it should be possible to keep fractious youngsters both enthralled and entertained.

One popular destination is the Piazza, where children will delight in feeding the pigeons (take along your own chunks of bread rather than buying expensive feed from the square's vendors). Then speed to the top of the Campanile for some truly magical views over the city. Other dizzying views can be seen from the campanile on San Giorgio dell Maggiore.

Most children find water and boats endlessly fascinating, and rides aboard the vaporetti are likely to prove highly popular. The constant toings and froings of gondolas, tugs, *traghetti* and other craft on the Grand Canal will also absorb many youngsters – and adults.

Museums which will appeal to children's imaginations are the Natural History Museum (see p.62), where some genuine monsters can be seen, and the Naval History Museum (see p.45), housing plenty of marvellous maritime artefacts, and complete ships to explore.

For more entertainment on a watery theme, visit the town's Aquarium, where the intriguing displays of lagoon, Adriatic and exotic marine life are bright and clear, as well as highly informative.

Excursions to the Lido for an exhilarating ride on the water banana or a more gentle pedalo promenade will prove invariably popular in summer.

Of course, children will also enjoy playing on the beaches, and older children or families may want to hire bicycles and pedal their way round the island. (Driving is permitted on the island, so watch out for traffic.) A trip to Murano to watch the glass blowers (see p.91) should captivate children of all ages.

Finally, if entertainment for the children is a priority, consider planning your trip to coincide with the Carnival (see p.105) or the Festa del Redentore fireworks in July (see p.103).

Eating Out

Although their city is not one of Italy's gastronomic capitals, Venetians are as enthusiastic as most Italians about food, and eating out is still an important occasion. Venice has a number of its own dishes and some very good local wines, and it also produces at least two excellent drinks.

Surprisingly perhaps for a city attracting such a vast, cosmopolitan crowd, restaurants in Venice serve almost exclusively Italian cuisine, and the vast majority of these focus on Venetian and other local dishes. There is, however, a scattering of Chinese restaurants and, around the Rialto, a few, quite avoidable fast-food outlets. International cuisine is usually found only in the most expensive hotel restaurants.

Where to Eat

For a selection of recommended restaurants in Venice, see our list starting on page 74. Eating establishments have a rather bewildering number of classifications, each suggesting different styles of service; *ristorante* implies high quality

---

Cicheti and Ombre

If you want to eat economically and try as many of the local goodies as possible, then look out for *osterie* and other bars serving *cicheti* (assorted snacks). Something akin to the Spanish tradition of *tapas*, these tasty morsels are displayed on the counter and can include everything from delicious garlic meatballs (*polpette*) to slices of fried vegetables, succulent seafood and mini-pizzas (*pizzete*).

To drink, order *una ombra* (literally 'shade') which will bring forth a glass of the house wine – always white unless you specify *rosso*. The name derives from the old civilized tradition of sitting in the Piazza in the shade to sip a glass of wine.

and expensive formality, while *trattoria* indicates straightforward dishes in a homely family atmosphere. In fact, many restaurants of all classes in Venice are still family concerns where most, if not all the food, is home-cooked (*casalinga*).

Other types of establishment include *locanda*, *osteria* and *taverna*. Don't be put off by the variety of names; simply let menu and price be your guide.

True *osterie* are the most characteristic and characterful of Venice's eating places. Part wine bar, part restaurant, they offer a modestly priced, limited menu (rarely translated into English) which is designed to cater for locals and more adventurous visitors.

Nearly all restaurants offer a *menù turistico*, a fixed-price three- or four-course menu with a limited choice of dishes. Although this may well appear to be a cheaper option when the same items are compared to *à la carte* prices, portions will invariably be smaller and the range of dishes is usually less interesting. If you are on a budget, you're better off look-

*F*ood with a view; served on the Grand Canal at the luxurious Hotel Bauer Grünwald.

ing for a *pizzeria*, where standard meals are often served in addition to pizzas. Try to pick one equipped with a traditional wood-burning oven for the very best flavours.

The majority of restaurants impose a cover and a service charge of between 10 and 15 percent, so there is no need to tip. Meal times are from noon to 2.30 or 3pm, while in the evening many restaurants close early, last orders usually being taken at around 10pm.

Venetian Cuisine

Venetians usually start the day with *colazione* – often little more than a coffee and a bread roll or croissant. Better hotels will offer a continental-style buffet and charge substantially extra for a cooked breakfast.

Both lunch (*pranzo*) and dinner (*cena*) generally offer a

choice of four courses: *antipasti* (starters or appetizers); *primi piatti* (first course); *secondi piatti* (second course) with *contorni* (vegetable or salad accompaniments); and finally *dessert* (dessert). Of course, you're not obliged to order all four courses.

Starters: typical *antipasti* include some of the following local favourites: *sarde in saor* (sardines and onions marinated in a mild vinaigrette sauce); *frutti di mare* (mixed seafood) comprising prawns, baby octopus and squid in a lemon and oil dressing; *vongole* or *capa-rozzoli* (clams) or *cozze* (mussels), often in a white wine sauce but also served with pasta as a *primi piatti*. A Venetian invention is *carpaccio*, thin slices of beef served with mayonnaise. *Antipasti* with meat include the ubiquitous *prosciutto* (ham) with melon (*melone*), also delicious with figs (*fichi*), as well as *affettato* or *salsicce* (charcuterie and salami-style sausage).

First Course: this is usually either pasta, risotto or soup. This far north, pasta generally gives way to rice and risotto is often recognized as *the* classic **111**

Venetian dish. Its constituents, apart from rice, are usually fresh vegetables (*primavera*) or seafood, the other local speciality. Venice's most famous pasta dish is bigoli in salsa (noodles in an anchovy or sardine sauce), but you won't find this on the menu everywhere. *Zuppa di pesce* (a stew-like fish soup) is usually a good choice. If you can't choose between pasta or soup, why not compromise on *pasta e fagioli*, a delicious thick, northern Italian pasta and white bean soup?

Fish: usually dominates the *secondi piatti*, and *grigliata dell'Adriatico* or *frittura/fritto misto* (Adriatic grill or mixed fried fish) are two favourite ways to sample the restaurant's piscean delights. Fish which occur frequently on the menu include *rombo* (turbot), *coda di rospo* (monkfish), *orata* (gilthead bream), *branzino/spigola* (sea-bass), *San Piero/sampiero* (John Dory) and *sfogio/sogliola* (which we know as sole).

Local seafood favourites are *granceola* (crab served in its own shell, often as an earlier course); *anguilla* (eel) – *alla veneziana* means it is cooked in a lemon, oil and tuna fish sauce; *seppie al nero* (cuttlefish in its own ink), a strange rich-tasting dish traditionally served with *polenta*, a firm, yellow cornmeal purée with no distinctive flavour which frequently accompanies the more richly sauced meals.

*C*olourful local produce is grown on the deserted islands and sold in the Rialto erberia.

Meat: the city's favourite is *fegato alla veneziana* (calf's liver with onions). This too is always served with *polenta*. *Vitello tonnato* (cold veal in tuna fish sauce) is also worth trying. Steak is a not so easy to track down in Venice. The best restaurants pride themselves on their Aberdeen Angus cuts, while *bistecca alla fiorentina* (Florentine T-bone steak) is Italy's finest if you can find it.

Vegetables: *contorni* generally include salads which feature *rucola* (rocket) and *radicchio*, both slightly bitter leaf varieties. Cooked vegetables often include a grilled assortment, while *carciofi* (artichokes) are a Venetian favourite.

Dessert: the choice is often limited to around half a dozen items, including the ubiquitous *gelato* (ice cream) and *tiramisù*, a spendid chilled confection of chocolate, coffee, cream or sweet *mascarpone* cheese and brandy. If you have the chance, do try *panna cotta* (literally, 'cooked cream'), which has a similar texture to crème caramel but a fresher, lighter taste. A typical Venetian custom is to serve *vino liquoroso con biscotti*, sweet biscuits or almond cake with a glass of dessert wine.

Cheese: the blue-veined *Gorgonzola* will probably be familiar, but it may surprise you to be offered *Parmigiano* or *Grana* (Parmesan). Among the Veneto province delicacies is a savoury, tangy goat's milk cheese named after the mountain town of Asiago, while other Italian varieties include the delicate *Bel Paese*.

Snacks

You don't need to splurge at lunch and dinner time. It's much cheaper to drop into one of the city's many bars or cafés for *tramezzini* (sandwiches), *panini* (baguette sandwiches), or *cicheti* (assorted snacks). If you sit down (generally waiter-service only), remember that food costs up to twice as much as if you order and stand at the bar. Sitting outside further increases the bill.

113

Drinks

Many **Veneto wines** are already familiar names as a result of their export success, including Soave, Valpolicella and Bardolino. Less familiar is the local wine region of Friuli, which supplies the good Pinot Grigio, for example, as well as several very palatable house wines (*vini della casa*). If you want to improve your knowledge, look out for an *enoteca*, a combination of wine bar and wine retailer.

Two sparkling drinks, consumed in cafés all over town, are **Prosecco**, a great sparkling white wine little seen outside the Veneto, and the universally renowned **spritzer**. Now recognized as a combination of wine and sparkling mineral water, the Venetians claim to have originated a slightly more potent version which includes a bitter such as Campari to give an extra kick. If this is too alcoholic, Campari can be substituted with the sweeter Select or the non-alcoholic Aperol.

Venice's other drink of note is the **Bellini**, an ambrosial concoction of champagne and fresh peach juice. It was invented by Signor Cipriani, the father of the current proprietor of Harry's Bar (Calle Vallaresso 1323, San Marco), the city's most famous (and most expensive) nightspot, but you'll also come across it elsewhere.

Venice has no after-dinner drinks to call its own, but you can still choose from the warm glow of **Vecchia Romagna** brandy, the sweet sensations of **Strega** or **Amaretto**, the anise taste of **Sambuca**, or the dubious delights of **Grappa** – Italy's firewater.

Non-alcoholic drinks include frothy hot chocolate in winter, and refreshing iced tea in summer. The best all-year-round drink is, of course, **coffee**. Black is *espresso*, while *cappuccino* is white and *caffè latte* is milky coffee served in a tall glass. Iced tea is served in summer from pre-mixed dispensers, flavoured with lemon (*al limone*) or peach (*alla pesca*). Mineral water (*acqua minerale*) is another popular drink with the locals – sparkling is *gasata*, still is *naturale*.

BLUEPRINT
for a
Perfect Trip

An A–Z Summary of Practical Information

A

ACCOMMODATION (See also CAMPING on p.118, YOUTH HOSTELS on p.139, and the list of RECOMMENDED HOTELS starting on p.65)

Accommodation in Venice ranges from some of Europe's finest five-star hotels along the waterfront to basic dormitories near the railway station. If there is any common factor it is that, like the city, they tend to be old and characterful.

As is the case in the rest of Europe, hotels (*alberghi*) are inspected regularly and graded from 5-star luxe to 1-star. A list of all hotels and prices is available from the tourist office.

As a general rule, the nearer to the Piazza, the more expensive the hotel. However, it is possible to find reasonably priced accommodation even in the district of San Marco. If you want something more economical, try looking across the Grand Canal in Dorsoduro rather than in the more downbeat area of the Lista di Spagna near the railway station. Except in the most exclusive five-star hotels, rates quoted are generally per room and include bed and continental breakfast. Air conditioning (essential in July and August) may be extra.

Advance booking is essential during the popular periods of spring and early summer, late summer and early autumn, around Christmas week and during Carnival, when prices are at their peak. However, in the chill of winter and sometimes during the sweltering period of July and August, it is relatively easy to find a room. Prices can drop by as much as 50 per cent in winter (though this may not begin until November) and prices may also be reduced in July and August.

There is a free hotel booking service at the railway station for hotels in Venice and another office just before the Ponte della Libertà which deals with hotels on the Lido. Note that many Lido hotels only open from April to October.

Below the category of 1-star hotels, there are a few hostels (*ostelli*) and dormitory accommodation which can be extremely economical. The tourist office can supply a list of such places.

There is very little self-catering accommodation in Venice; enquire at the tourist office for details.

If you have to check out of your room several hours before your flight home and wish to freshen up, it's worth noting that there is a day hotel (*albergo diurno*) just off the Piazza, behind the *Ala Napoleonica*, where you can have a shower and leave belongings.

I'd like a single/double room.	**Vorrei una camera singola/matrimoniale.**
with (without) bath/shower	**con (senza) bagno/doccia**
What's the rate per night?	**Qual è il prezzo per una notte?**

AIRPORT (*aeroporto*)

Venice Marco Polo is the main airport, 13km (8 miles) north of the city. Occasionally, charter flights use **Treviso,** 30km (18 miles) north.

Ground transfer. Public buses (ACTV) run from the airport to the Piazzale Roma terminus about once an hour in winter and every half-hour in summer. Airport buses (ATVO) have a similar timetable but are timed more to coincide with major airline departures and arrivals. Both are inexpensive (the ACTV service is the cheaper) and take around 20 minutes to get to Piazzale Roma. Buy your tickets from the general souvenir shop.

Once at Piazzale Roma, look out for the beginning of the Grand Canal behind the bus terminus. Board the No. 1 *vaporetto* (waterbus) for an all-stages ride along the Grand Canal or a No. 82 if you want the quickest route to San Marco.

Boat transfer. Motorboats of the Cooperativa San Marco provide an all-year-round direct service between the airport and San Marco (stopping at the Lido) at about twice the cost of the combined ATVO/*vaporetto* trip. It's still relatively inexpensive, however, and if **117**

the *vaporetti* are busy and you have a lot of baggage, it's well worth the extra lire. (Don't confuse the Cooperativa San Marco service with the terribly expensive water-taxi service – *motoscafi* – which uses similar craft for the transfer.) The service runs every 60-90 minutes and departs from just outside the airport building. There is a ticket office in the arrivals lobby (buy your return ticket by the dock at the San Marco quayside).

Airport facilities. You'll find all the usual amenities of an international airport, including bar, restaurant (just outside the terminal), bank and currency-exchange office (*cambio*), souvenir and general shops and a small duty-free shop. There are also hotel and tourist information booths. Assistance for wheelchair travellers is available and there are toilets for disabled visitors.

If you do fly into Treviso airport, take the No. 6 bus into the centre of Treviso from where there are frequent coach and rail connections to Venice.

Where's the boat/bus for …?	**Dove si prende il vaporetto/ l'autobus per…?**
I want a ticket to Piazzale Roma.	**Desidero uno biglietto per Piazzale Roma**.

CAMPING (*campeggio*) (See also ROLLING VENICE on p.131)
There is no camping in Venice and the nearest recommended site is on the Lido, though you will need your own tent to camp here. There are several sites on the mainland and some also offer bungalow and caravan accommodation. The tourist office may be able to provide details (see p.135).

Compared to a hostel, camping is not a particularly cheap option, and many of the sites (apart from the Lido) are not in very attractive or convenient locations.

May we camp here?   **Possiamo campeggiare qui?**

CLIMATE and CLOTHING

Simply put, winters are cold, summers are hot and the rest of the year is pleasantly in between. The winds off the Adriatic and occasional flooding means that Venice can be a damp and chilly (though always atmospheric) place between November and March. During the month of June the temperature starts to rise and July and August can be stifling. Air conditioning is essential to ensure a good night's rest at this time of year. Below is a chart showing average monthly air temperatures in Venice:

		J	F	M	A	M	J	J	A	S	O	N	D
Max.	°F	42	46	54	63	71	77	83	83	79	65	54	46
	°C	6	8	12	17	22	25	28	28	26	18	12	8
Min.	°F	34	34	41	51	57	64	68	66	62	52	43	37
	°C	1	1	5	10	14	18	20	19	17	11	6	3

Clothing. The most important thing to pack at any time of year is comfortable walking shoes. Despite Venice's good canal transport network, you'll be spending most of your time on foot.

During summer you'll need thin cotton clothing and, from June to September, it's a good idea to take a jumper or jacket for cooler evenings. Do remember to cover up your back and shoulders when sightseeing in churches and that shorts above knee length are prohibited. Although few churches actually enforce this dress code, you will definitely not be allowed to flout it in St Mark's Basilica.

In winter, wrap up well and consider bringing good waterproof footwear to cope with the floodwaters. Many Venetians go around in knee boots (you can always buy a pair on the spot quite reasonably if the flooding is bad).

Venice is an informal city but, in the best restaurants, something dressy is appropriate, especially during the indoor season. Men will feel underdressed without a tie in the Fenice theatre and in the casino a jacket and tie are essential for entry.

COMMUNICATIONS (See also Opening Hours on p.132 and Time Differences on p.134)

Post Offices (*posta/ufficio postale*). The main office can be found on Fondaco dei Tedeschi at Rialto while the two main sub-offices are on the Zattere in Dorsoduro and Calle dell'Ascensione just off the Piazza. These handle mail and telegrams and the Rialto has public telephones. The lobby of the main office can be used 24 hours a day for telegrams, faxes, and express and registered letters.

Post boxes are red. Postage stamps are also sold at tobacconists (*tabacchi*), marked by a distinctive 'T' sign.

Poste restante (general delivery). If you wish to use this service, then have mail addressed to you care of: Fermo Posta, Posta Centrale, Rialto, Venice, Italy. Don't forget your passport when you come to collect your mail.

I'd like a stamp for this letter/postcard.	**Desidero un francobollo per questa lettera/cartolina.**
express (special delivery)	**espresso**
airmail	**via aerea**
registered	**raccomandata**
I want to send a telegram to …	**Desidero mandare un telegramma a …**

Telephones (*telefono*). You can make international calls from the Telecom office (pay after your call), or at one of the several easy-to-use phone booths dotted around the city. You can also call from several bars or cafés – look for the telephone symbol outside.

Telephones take coins, credit-style cards (*scheda telefonica* – available in denominations of L.5,000 and L.10,000) or tokens (*gettoni*), though the latter are a now a dying breed.

The cheapest rates are between 11pm and 8am Monday to Friday and 11pm and 2pm Saturday and Sunday.

Some useful numbers:

Domestic directory enquiries (information)   **12**
Operator for Europe   **15**
Operator for intercontinental calls   **170**

Direct dialling codes: **Australia** 0061; **Canada**: 001, **Republic of Ireland**: 00353; **South Africa**: 0027; **UK**: 0044; **USA**: 001. (Don't forget to omit the first zero from your local code.)

COMPLAINTS

There should be little cause for complaint in Venice. Prices of goods, meals, drinks and accommodation as well as gondola fares and other service charges are either fixed by the authorities or advertised in advance. If you do have a complaint, however, the best thing to do is to try and resolve any problems directly. If this fails, take your grievance to the tourist office. For serious complaints, go to the *questura* (police headquarters) on the Fondamente San Lorenzo in Castello.

CRIME (See also EMERGENCIES on p.123 and POLICE on p.132)

Venice is one of the safest cities in Italy, and cases of violence involving tourists are extremely rare. Though women may be pestered, such attention is unlikely to escalate beyond controllable bounds. Petty thieves operate here as in all tourist centres, and you should be particularly careful of your belongings on crowded *vaporetti* and in the busy streets between the Piazza and the Rialto. It's wise to leave unneeded documents and excess money locked up at the hotel.

I want to report a theft.   **Voglio denunciare un furto.**

CUSTOMS (*dogana*) and ENTRY FORMALITIES

Any citizen of the European Union (EU) holding a valid passport may stay for an unrestricted time in Italy. Visitors from Australia, New Zealand, the USA and South Africa may stay up to three months without a visa. When you check into your hotel your passport details are registered with the police. If you are self-catering or staying in private accommodation, you should go and register at the police headquarters (see POLICE on p.132).

121

Duty-free allowance. As Italy is part of the EU (formerly EC), free exchange of non-duty free goods for personal use is permitted between Italy, the UK and the Republic of Ireland (residents only). However, duty-free items are still subject to restrictions: check before you go. For residents of non-EU countries, restrictions on entering their own country are as follows: **Australia**: 250 cigarettes **or** 250g tobacco; 1l alcohol. **Canada**: 200 cigarettes **and** 50 cigars **and** 400g tobacco; 1.1l spirits **or** wine **or** 8.5l beer; **New Zealand**: 200 cigarettes **or** 50 cigars **or** 250g tobacco; 4.5l wine **or** beer **and** 1.1l spirits. **South Africa**: 400 cigarettes **and** 50 cigars **and** 250g tobacco; 2l wine **and** 1l spirits. **USA**: 200 cigarettes **and** 2kg of tobacco **and** 100 cigars (not Cuban).

Currency restrictions. As a foreign tourist you may import up to a maximum of L.400,000 in cash and you must declare if you intend taking out in excess of L.20,000,000, or its foreign equivalent.

I've nothing to declare. **Non ho nulla da dichiarare.**

D

DRIVING

Venice is a **traffic-free zone** and the closest you can get in a car is the Piazzale Roma, where there are two large multi-level car parks. A huge multi-storey car park can also be found on the adjacent car-park island of Tronchetto, connected by *vaporetto* to the city centre. Tronchetto is also the terminal for the car ferry to the Lido where driving is allowed. The two car parks at Mestre San Giuliano and Fusina operate only during Easter, summer and Carnival. Although the outdoor car parks are meant to be guarded night and day, it's sensible not to leave anything of value in your car. In the indoor garages you must leave your doors unlocked and the key in the ignition. There are left-luggage (baggage-check) facilities at Piazzale Roma.

Note that parking is expensive and if the Veneto is the only area you intend to explore outside Venice, you should consider getting about by public transport.

ELECTRIC CURRENT

220-volt current is supplied to all but the oldest of Venice's areas. Take along a European adaptor for your appliances.

What's the voltage, 220 or 110?	**Qual è il voltaggio, 220 (duecentoventi) o 110 (centodieci)?**
I'd like an adaptor/ a battery.	**Vorrei una presa complementare/una batteria.**

EMBASSIES and CONSULATES (*ambasciata; consolato*)

Most consulates are open from Monday to Friday from about 9am to 5pm but close for lunch.

Australia (embassy): Via Alessandria, 215, Rome; tel. (06) 83 27 21.
Canada (embassy): Via GB de Rossi, 27, Rome; tel. (06) 841 53 41.
Republic of Ireland (embassy): Largo del Nazzareno, 3, Rome; tel. (06) 678 25 41.
South Africa (embassy): Via Tanaro, 14-16, Rome; tel. (06) 841 97 94.
UK (consulate): Palazzo Querini, Dorsoduro, 1051, Venice; tel. (041) 522 72 07.
USA (consulate): Largo Donegani, 1, Milan; tel. (02) 29 03 51.

EMERGENCIES (See also EMBASSIES AND CONSULATES, above, MEDICAL CARE on p.129 and POLICE on p.132)

Here are the important numbers to call:

All services	**113**
Police	**112**
Ambulance	**523 00 00**
Fire	**115**

In the highly unlikely event that you see someone fall overboard from a *vaporetto*, shout '*uomo in mare!*' ('man overboard!') and throw the person the nearest lifebelt.

Careful!	**Attenzione!**
Fire!	**Incendio!**
Help (police)!	**Polizia!**
Stop!	**Stop!**
Stop! Thief!	**Al ladro!**

ETIQUETTE

Venetians are generally friendly, polite, outgoing (though less exuberant than their fellow countrymen) and many are quite eager to communicate in English. They are justly proud of their city, and a good way to start up a conversation is to comment enthusiastically on what you have seen of Venice, especially if it is somewhere off the usual tourist route.

You won't meet many locals around the Piazza or the Rialto Bridge, which both seethe with tourists in high season; try instead the squares of Santa Margherita in Dorsoduro or San Bartolomeo and San Luca in San Marco, which are popular meeting spots for young locals. Some common greetings are listed on pp.126-7.

GAY and LESBIAN TRAVELLERS

Venice has few obviously gay meeting points, limited in part by its restricted nightlife. One such is *Paradiso Perduto* on Fondamenta della Misericordia in Cannaregio. In the same district, on Calle Lionpardo (off Rio Terrà San Leonardo), *La Casa Gialla* is a women-only weekend disco.

GUIDES (*guida*) and TOURS

The tourist office (see p.135) will supply you with a list of qualified tour guides if you would like a personal tour of a particular site or on any specialist aspect of Venice.

A number of standard tours are run throughout the year and can be booked through your hotel or via most travel agencies. These include a two-hour **walking tour** of San Marco, taking in the basilica, the Doges' Palace and a glass-blowing workshop, a two-hour **walking and gondola tour** covering the Frari and the Grand Canal, a one-hour evening gondola serenade and a three-hour **islands tour**. These tours are generally expensive and all can be done much more economically under your own steam.

A **cruise** to Padua aboard the *Burchiello*, a 200-seater motorboat, makes for an interesting, though expensive, day out. There are several splendid 17th- and 18th-century villas to admire along the way, two of which are visited as part of the tour. The return journey to Venice is by coach.

When visiting **churches** make sure you have enough small change to operate the multilingual, telephone-style, taped commentaries available and to turn on the lights to illuminate important paintings.

Free tours are given of the basilica in summer, while a 'Secret Tour' (*Itinerari Segreti*) will show you the ins and outs of life behind the public scenes at the Doges' Palace.

Evening lectures on the **art and history** of Venice ('for the short-term visitor') are held on Wednesday, Thursday and Friday (Apr-Oct) in the building adjoining the church at Campo Santa Maria Formosa, 5254. Pick up a leaflet from your hotel or the tourist office.

L

LANGUAGE

All Venetian hotels above a basic standard have staff who speak some English, French or German and, unless you go well off the beaten track, you should have no problem communicating in shops or restaurants. In bars and cafés away from the Piazza, however, you'll almost certainly have an opportunity to practise your Italian, and the locals will think more of you for making the effort.

Remember that the letter 'c' is pronounced 'ch' (as in church) when it is followed by 'e' or 'i', while 'ch' is a hard sound pronounced like the 'c' in cat. You'll often hear waiters using the term '*Prego*' to mean 'Can I take your order?'. The all-purpose, friendly '*ciao*', meaning hello or goodbye, should not be used on formal occasions, but it probably won't take long before a Venetian greets you (or bids you farewell) with it, in which case it's absolutely fine to return the compliment.

Venetians have a dialect that is quite distinct from the rest of Italy, though to the visitor unfamiliar with the Italian language, this is somewhat academic. However, you may notice that both Venetian and Italian names are used in street signs and on maps, for example San Giuliano is slurred to San Zulian, Santi Giovanni e Paolo is San Zanipolo, Giovanni becomes Zani and so on.

You will find a list of useful expressions on the cover of this guide. The Berlitz ITALIAN PHRASE BOOK & DICTIONARY covers most situations you are likely to encounter, while the Berlitz Italian-English/English-Italian pocket dictionary will fill in any gaps and also contains a menu-reader supplement.

Good morning/afternoon	**Buon giorno**
Good evening/Good night	**Buona sera/Buona notte**
Goodbye	**Arrivederci**
How are you?	**Come sta?**
Very well thanks, and you?	**Molto bene, grazie, e lei?**
Excuse me.	**Mi scusi.**
Excuse me (may I pass?)	**Permesso?**
You're welcome.	**Prego.**
where/when/how?	**dove/quando/come?**
yesterday/today/tomorrow	**ieri/oggi/domani**

day/week/month/year	**giorno/settimana/mese/anno**
left/right	**sinistra/destra**
up/down	**su/giù**
good/bad	**buono/cattivo**
big/small	**grande/piccolo**
cheap/expensive	**buon mercato/caro**
hot/cold	**caldo/freddo**
old/new	**vecchio/nuovo**
early/late	**presto/tardi**
free (vacant)/occupied	**libero/occupato**
near/far	**vicino/lontano**
early/late	**presto/tardi**
full/empty	**pieno/vuoto**
Waiter/waitress, please.	**Cameriere!/Cameriera!** or **Senta!** (= 'listen')

LAUNDRY and DRY CLEANING (*lavanderia; tintoria*)

Venice has only a few laundries and cleaners but they're worth seeking out on an extended stay as hotel cleaning charges are expensive. Look in the Yellow Pages, ask your hotel receptionist or try the ones in Campiello di Salizzada del Pistor (near the church of San Apostoli), or on Fondamente Pescaria, off Rio Terrà San Leonardo – both in Cannaregio.

The prices are the same whether you do the washing yourself or leave it with an attendant.

When will it be ready?	**Quando sarà pronto?**
I must have this for tomorrow morning.	**Mi serve per domani mattina.**

LOST PROPERTY (*oggetti rinvenuti*)

Venetians are noted for their honesty and this is one of the few cities in Europe where your lost property may turn up. (Go back to the bar where you left your sunglasses or books and they'll invariably be behind the counter waiting for you.) If you lose something on a *vaporetto*, there's a lost property office in the ACTV building next to the San Angelo stop on the Grand Canal.

There are also lost property offices at the airport and railway station, while the general lost property office, the *Ufficio all'Economato*, is housed in Ca'Farsetti on Calle Loredan near the Rialto Bridge.

MEDIA

Radio and TV (*radio; televisione*). Shortwave reception is good and BBC World Service and Voice of America can be easily picked up. After dark the American Armed Forces Network (AFN) from Frankfurt or Munich can be heard on regular AM radio (middle or medium wave). RAI broadcasts only in Italian but many hotels now subscribe to satellite channels showing pan-European programmes.

Newspapers and Magazines (*giornale, rivista*). Some British and other foreign-language newspapers are on sale at the airport, the railway station and at news-stands near the Rialto Bridge and the Piazza, arriving the day after publication.

The local papers *Gazzettino* and *Nuova Venezia* both have listings, but the most useful publication is *Un Ospite di Venezia* which comes out fortnightly and is available free in many hotels or from the tourist office. This gives listings for all visitor attractions, events and exhibitions including opening times and prices and also has a useful section on practical information.

Have you any English-language newspapers? **Avete giornali in inglese?**

MEDICAL CARE (See also Emergencies on p.123)

No vaccinations are needed and there are no specific ailments to worry about in Venice, but it is advisable to take out a holiday health insurance policy. European Community countries have a reciprocal agreement with Italy which entitles all visitors from other EC countries to treatment by the national health services under the same terms and conditions as residents – ask your local health centre ahead for your trip for more details.

Mosquitoes can be a nuisance in summer though they are by no means as common as the presence of so much water might lead you to think. Take along the small, plug-in machine which burns a tablet emitting fumes noxious to mosquitoes. Airport shops sell these and some hotels also provide them.

The main hospital (*ospedale*) is next to San Zanipolo church and many doctors speak English. The number of the first-aid section (*pronto soccorso*) is **523 00 00/529 45 17**.

Chemists (*farmacia*) are open during normal shop hours and rotate for night and holiday cover service. The address of the nearest open chemist is posted on the door of the others. Night chemists (*farmacie di turno*) are also listed in *Un Ospite di Venezia* (see Media, opposite); alternatively, you can telephone **192**.

I need a doctor/dentist.	**Ho bisogno di un medico/ un dentista.**
I've a pain here.	**Ho un dolore qui.**
a stomach ache	**il mal di stomaco**
a fever	**la febbre**

MONEY MATTERS
(See also Customs and Entry Formalities on p.121)

Currency. The *lira* (plural *lire*, abbreviated L. or Lit.) is Italy's monetary unit.
Coins: L.50, 100, 200, 500.
Banknotes: L.1,000, 2,000, 5,000, 10,000, 50,000, 100,000.

Exchange facilities. Banks are the cheapest option and the transaction is usually rapid and courteous. Rates are not fixed but do not vary greatly. Commission is small so it's not worth shopping around. Don't forget to take along your passport when changing travellers' cheques. Exchange offices (*cambio*) are an alternative out of banking hours, while the most expensive option is your hotel. Automatic currency exchange machines can also be found.

Credit cards and travellers' cheques are accepted in most places, though you may not get a favourable rate when paying by the latter.

PLANNING YOUR BUDGET

To give you an idea of what to expect, here are some average prices in Italian lire. However, prices can only be approximate as inflation creeps relentlessly up. Note that prices marked with an asterisk are fixed by the Venetian authorities; you should check these in the latest edition of *Un Ospite di Venezia* (see MEDIA on p.128).

Airport transfer. *By road*: public bus (ACTV) L.1,200, airport bus (ATVO) L.5,000, taxi L.40,000-45,000 (max. 4 people) plus L.1-2,000 per piece of luggage. *By water*: motorboat (Cooperativa San Marco) L.15,000, private taxi L.100,000-120,000 (max. 4 people).

Camping (per person per night). Tent L.9,500, bungalow or caravan L.15,000.

Entertainment. Casino L.5,000 (access to slot machines), L.15,000 (access to all tables), disco L.15,000-20,000 (including first drink), folklore evening L.34,000.

Gondolas*. Daytime rate L.80,000 for 50 minutes (up to 5 people), L.40,000 for each subsequent 25 minutes. Evening rate L.100,000 for 50 minutes (from 8pm to 8am).

Guided tours. For a walking tour, allow L.33,000; walking/gondola tour L.30,000; half-day islands tour 25,000; gondola serenade L.40,000; *Burchiello* to Padua L.108,000 (excluding lunch).

Hotels (bed and breakfast per night in high season inclusive of tax). 5-star L.400,000 and over, 4-star L.250-400,000, 3-star L.165-250,000, 2-star L.100-160,000.

Lido beach. Entrance to Hotel Des Bains beach L.19,500, beach cabins L.120-180,000 per day.

Meals and drinks. Three-course meal per person in a reasonable establishment, including cover and service, excluding drinks, L.40-60,000, pizza L.10-15,000. In a café or bar (standing up): sandwich L.1,500-3,500, ice cream L.1,500-3,000, coffee L.1,300-2,500, soft drink L.2,500. Alcoholic drinks: beer L.3,000, glass of house wine L.1,000, spritzer L.1,800.

Museums and attractions. Museums and galleries L.3-6,000, Doges' Palace L.12,000, Accademia L.12,000, Guggenheim Collection L.10,000, Scuola Grande di San Rocco L.8,000, Biennale L.15,000; *biglietto cumulativo* (access to the Doges' Palace, Museo Correr, Ca'Pésaro, Ca'Rezzonico and Murano's Museo Vetrario) L.25,000 (saving about L.15,000 on individual entrance fees).

Porters luggage charge*. Up to a distance of 50m L.1,500 per piece; 51-300m L.2,000 per piece; above 300m, 1 piece L4,000, additional piece L.3,000. Maximum charge between any two points (excluding Tronchetto and islands) for 1-2 pieces L.9,000, each additional piece L.3,000.

Transport. *Vaporetto*: uninterrupted travel L.4,000-7,200 (return), 24-hour ticket L.15,000, 72-hour ticket L.30,000, weekly ticket L.55,000. *Motoscafo* (water taxi) Piazzale Roma to San Marco L.70,000.

ROLLING VENICE

If you or someone in your party is aged between 14 and 30 and you are visiting during summer or Carnival, then enrol with the official youth-oriented discount scheme known as 'Rolling Venice'. For a fee of L.5,000, you are entitled to discounts on 25 museums and galleries, 72-hour *vaporetto* tickets, as well as shopping, restaurants and accommodation. As you are able to more than recoup your fee simply by visiting the Guggenheim Collection, the Scuola Grande di San Rocco and the Scuola di San Giorgio, joining the scheme makes very good financial sense. Enrol at the offices in the railway station or at the back of the Piazza. Directions are affixed to the door of the main tourist information office (look for the sign '*Assessorato alla Gioventù*' in Corte Contarina, rather than 'Rolling Venice').

OPENING HOURS (See also PUBLIC HOLIDAYS on p.133)

Banks. Hours are from 8.30am to 1.30pm and from 3 to 4pm Monday to Friday.

Bars and restaurants. Some café-bars open for breakfast while others wait until around noon. The vast majority close early, around 10.30 to 11pm. Nearly all restaurants close for at least one day per week and some close for parts of August, January and February.

Churches. Most open from around 8am to noon and from 3 or 4pm until 6 or 7pm Monday to Saturday. On Sunday some open only for services in the morning.

Museums and galleries. Most close on one day of the week, usually Monday, and open from 9 or 10am to around 6pm. Some open only during the morning. (See also p.41.)

Post offices. The main office, Fondaco dei Tedeschi, is open from 8.15am to 7pm, while main branches on Calle dell'Ascensione and Zattere open from 8.10am to 1.25pm Monday to Friday, 8.10am to noon on Saturday.

Shops. Business hours are from 8 or 9am to 1pm and from 3-4pm to 7pm Monday to Saturday. Some tourist shops are open on Sunday.

P

POLICE (*polizia, carabinieri*) (See also EMERGENCIES on p.123)
You rarely see them and very rarely need them but Venice's police-men function efficiently and are courteous to foreign visitors.

For serious matters telephone the *carabinieri*; the switchboard should be able to find someone who speaks your language. Telephone **113** in an emergency.

Where's the nearest police station?	**Dov'è il più vicino posto di polizia?**
I am lost.	**Mi sono perso(a).**

PUBLIC HOLIDAYS (*festa*)

Italy has nine public holidays a year. When one falls on a Thursday or a Tuesday, many Italians make a *ponte* (bridge) to the weekend, taking off Friday and Monday as well.

1 January	**Capodanno** or **Primo dell'Anno**	New Year's Day
6 January	**Epifania**	Epiphany
25 April	**Festa della Liberazione**	Liberation Day
1 May	**Festa del Lavoro**	Labour Day
25 August	**Ferragosto**	Assumption Day
1 November	**Ognissanti**	All Saint's Day
8 December	**Immacolata Concezione**	Immaculate Conception
25 December	**Natale**	Christmas Day
26 December	**Santo Stefano**	St Stephen's Day
Movable date	**Lunedi di Pasqua**	Easter Monday

The Festa della Salute on 21 November is a local holiday when many shops close for the day.

R

RELIGION

Roman Catholic mass in Venice's churches is normally celebrated only in Italian, but confessions are heard daily in several languages at the Basilica di San Marco in summer. See the publication *Un Ospite di Venezia* for times (see MEDIA on p.128).

Non-catholic services are held at the following churches:
Anglican. Church of St George, Campo San Vio, Dorsoduro.
Evangelical Lutheran. Campo Santi Apostoli, Cannaregio.
Evangelical Waldensian and **Methodist**. Santa Maria Formosa, Castello.
Greek Orthodox. Ponte dei Greci, Castello.
Jewish Synagogue. Ghetto Vecchio, Cannaregio.

What time is the mass/ service?	**A che ora è la messa/la funzione?**
Is it in English?	**È in inglese?**

TIME DIFFERENCES
Italy follows Central European Time (GMT + 1) and from late March to late September clocks are put one hour ahead (GMT + 2). The following chart indicates time differences during the summer:

New York	London	**Italy**	Jo'burg	Sydney	Auckland
6am	11am	**noon**	noon	8pm	10pm

What time is it?	**Che ore sono?**

TIPPING
As a service charge is added to most restaurant bills (sometimes as much as 15 percent) it is not necessary to tip as well. Do, however, tip bell-boys, the elderly gondolier posted at the landing station who helps you into and out of your craft, and tour guides. It is also customary to give a small tip to toilet/restroom attendants.

Hotel porter, per bag	L.1,000
Hotel maid, per day	L.1,000-2,000
Toilet attendant	L.300
Keep the change.	**Tenga il resto**.

TOILETS/RESTROOMS

Most museums and galleries have public toilets of a reasonable standard. You can also use the facilities in restaurants, bars and cafés, but it is polite to order a drink of some sort in return.

There are public toilets in the airport, railway station, car parks and the following popular locations: the *alberghi diurni* (day hotels) just off the Piazza (there may be long queues), in front of the Accademia, and off Campo San Bartolomeo near San Martino church. There is a standard charge of L.500.

Where are the toilets?   **Dove sono i gabinetti?**

TOURIST INFORMATION OFFICES

The Italian State Tourist Board (ENIT) has several offices abroad, and can provide general information, lists of accommodation and helpful brochures in advance of your trip.

Australia & New Zealand	ENIT, c/o Alitalia, Orient Overseas Building, Suite 202, 32 Bridge Street, Sydney, NSW 2000; tel. (2) 271-308
Canada	1, Place Ville-Marie, Suite 1914, Montreal, Quebec H3B 3M9; tel. (514) 866-7667
United Kingdom & Eire	1, Princes Street, London W1R 8AY, tel. (0171) 408 1254
USA	401 N Michigan Avenue, Suite 3030, Chicago 1, IL 60611; tel (312) 644-0966
	ENIT, c/o Italian Trade Commission, 499 Park Avenue, New York, NY 1022; tel. (212) 843-6884/6885
	12400 Wilshire Boulevard, Suite 550, Los Angeles CA 90025; tel. (310) 820-0098

Tourist information offices in Venice:
The main office is at San Marco, Palazzetto Selva, Giardinetti Reali (Royal Gardens); tel. 522 63 56 or 529 87 30.

There are other offices at Piazzale Roma, the railway station, the airport and the Lido (Gran Viale; tel. 76 57 21).

TRANSPORT

Waterbuses. The only public transport in Venice is water-borne. An efficient system of **vaporetti** (waterbuses) will take you to within a short walk of anywhere you want to get to in the city. However, Venice is so compact that for short journeys it is often quicker to walk. *Vaporetti* ply the Grand Canal, go round to the north shore of the city (where the main stop is Fondamente Nuove) and shuttle to and from the other islands. They are inexpensive and provide a wonderful perspective on the city.

Buy your ticket in advance from the ticket offices on or close to the landing stages at the main stops, or at any shop displaying an ACTV sign. There is a flat tariff for each line, irrespective of the number of stops you travel. A 24-hour or 72-hour pass is a worthwhile investment if you intend seeing much of the city (or if you want to use the *vaporetti* simply to hop across the Grand Canal).

You must validate your ticket by stamping it at the machine on the landing stage. If you haven't bought a ticket before boarding, buy one immediately on board from the *vaporetto* conductor. A small surcharge is payable.

The main service is the No. 1 (*accelerato*) which stops at every stage along the Grand Canal. The No. 82 (*diretto*) goes direct from the car park Tronchetto-Piazzale Roma-Railway Station-Gran Canal Rialto to San Marco and the Lido. The No. 12 runs from Fondamente Nuove to Murano, Burano and Torcello.

If you intend taking the No. 52 (*circolare*) to the north shore, note that it goes from the Riva degli Schiavoni, San Zaccaria, via the Arsenal Fondamenta Nuove to Murano, proceeding clockwise the long way round to Piazzale Roma-Canale della Giudecca-San Zaccaria and the Lido.

Water taxis. If you need a door-to-door service or you'd simply prefer to move in more refined, less crowded circles, ask your hotel to call you a *motoscafo*. They are fast but extremely expensive.

Gondolas. These are no longer a means of public transport, but anyone can take a cheap gondola ride on the *traghetto* (ferry) service at various points across the Grand Canal.

TRAVELLERS WITH DISABILITIES

Venice is not as inaccessible as it might seem. An excellent free map and leaflet has been compiled by an organization known as *Venezia per Tutti* (Venice for All), giving details of those areas of the city accessible to wheelchair-users. The organization can also advise blind and partially sighted visitors of any attractions with appropriate facilities.

The key to getting about is the use of *vaporetti* to circumvent the 411 footbridges which link Venice's 120 mini-islands. Virtually all *vaporetti* are adapted to take wheelchairs and the area between the *vaporetto* stop and the next footbridge is accessible. The only drawback is low water which causes a step up to the landing platform, and choppy waters are hazardous in winter. Some footbridges are being installed with lifts, but as yet only a handful are in operation.

The map and leaflet also detail accessible accommodation and visitor attractions as well as toilet facilities for the disabled. Accessible attractions include the basilica, the Doges' Palace, the Ca' Rezzonico, the churches of the Frari, San Zanipolo, Salute and San Giorgio Maggiore as well as several museums. However, no differentiation is made between full access and partial access.

For a free copy of the map, write in advance to the tourist office or pick one up at the office of the ULSS, 16, Piazzale Roma. For general advice before leaving Britain contact RADAR, 12 City Forum, 250 City Road, London EC1V 8AF, tel. (0171) 250 3222. In the USA contact Mobility International USA, PO Box 3551, Eugene, OR 97403; tel (503) 343-1284, or the Society for the Advancement of Travel for the Handicapped, 347 Fifth Avenue, Suite 610, New York, NY 10016; tel. (212) 447-7284.

TRAVELLING TO VENICE (See also AIRPORT on p.117)

By air. Venice Marco Polo airport is on several European scheduled routes, though travellers from further afield will have to change at a European gateway or a major Italian city. Charter flights occasionally land at Treviso, 30km (18 miles) north. Flights from the USA require a change at Rome or Milan (the flight time from Milan to Venice is about 45 minutes).

By rail. The journey by train from London to Venice takes 27 hours (less with Le Shuttle) and is no cheaper than a late-availability charter flight. From Paris the TGV travels to Lausanne, where passengers should change for a 10-hour journey to Venice via Milan.

If Venice forms part of your Grand Tour, enquire about an Inter-Rail Pass (available to European residents only) which gives one month's unlimited travel within Continental Europe and discounts on British rail travel. For non-European residents there is a similar Eurailpass (not valid for travel within Britain) which must be purchased before leaving home.

Finally, if money is no obstacle, then arrive in style aboard the Venice Simplon-Orient Express, departing from London up to twice a week between late March and early November; telephone (071) 620 0003 for details.

By road. The main access roads to Venice are via Basle-St Gotthard-Milan, or via Le Shuttle from London to Paris on to Geneva-Mont Blanc-Milan. You can travel by motorail either from Boulogne or Paris to Milan or via Basle and Chiasso.

WATER (acqua)

Venice's tap water is perfectly safe to drink and so too is the water from the drinking fountains you will see around the city. In cases where tap water is not drinkable it will be marked with the sign *acqua non potabile.*

Most natives drink copious quantities of mineral water (*acqua minerale*) and a glass for water is always set on the restaurant table.

half-litre/litre of
mineral water

**un mezzo litro/litro di
acqua minerale**

WEIGHTS and MEASURES

Length

Temperature

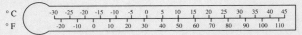

Weight

grams	0	100	200	300	400	500	600	700	800	900	. 1 kg
ounces	0	4	8	12	1 lb	20	24	28	2 lb		

WOMEN TRAVELLERS
Venice is one of the very few European cities in which it is safe for women to walk alone at night. Women-only dormitory accommodation can be found at the Instituto Suore Canossiane at Ponte Piccolo, 428, Giudecca; tel. 522 21 57.

Y

YOUTH HOSTELS (*ostello della gioventù*)
Venice's only International Youth Hostel Federation-approved hostel is an atmospheric old building on Giudecca at Fondamente Zitelle (tel. 523 82 11). However, there are several hostels and places offering cheap accommodation. Ask the tourist office (see p.135) for a list.

Index

Where there is more than one set of references, the one in **bold** refers to the main entry, the one in *italics* to an illustration.

141

Other Berlitz titles include:

Africa
Kenya
Morocco
South Africa
Tunisia

Asia, Middle East
Bali and Lombok
China
Egypt
Hong Kong
India
Indonesia
Israel
Japan
Malaysia
Singapore
Sri Lanka
Thailand

Australasia
Australia
New Zealand
Sydney

Austria, Switzerland
Austrian Tyrol
Switzerland
Vienna

Belgium, The Netherlands
Amsterdam
Bruges and Ghent
Brussels

British Isles
Channel Islands
Dublin
Edinburgh
Ireland
London
Scotland

Caribbean, Latin America
Bahamas
Bermuda
Cancún and Cozumel

Cuba
French West Indies
Jamaica
Mexico
Puerto Rico
Southern Caribbean
Virgin Islands

Central and Eastern Europe
Budapest
Czech Republic
Moscow and St Petersburg
Prague

France
Brittany
Côte d'Azur
Dordogne
Euro Disney Resort
France
Normandy
Paris
Provence

Germany
Berlin
Munich

Greece, Cyprus and Turkey
Athens
Corfu
Crete
Cyprus
Greek Islands
Istanbul
Rhodes
Turkey

Italy and Malta
Florence
Italy
Malta
Milan and the Lakes
Naples
Rome
Sicily
Venice

North America
Boston
California
Canada
Disneyland and the Theme Parks of Southern California
Florida
Hawaii
Los Angeles
New Orleans
New York
San Francisco
USA
Walt Disney World and Orlando
Washington D.C.

Portugal
Algarve
Lisbon
Madeira
Portugal

Scandinavia
Copenhagen
Helsinki
Oslo and Bergen
Stockholm
Sweden

Spain
Barcelona
Canary Islands
Costa Blanca
Costa del Sol
Costa Dorada and Tarragona
Ibiza and Formentera
Madrid
Mallorca and Menorca
Spain

Special
Channel Hopper's Wine Guide (UK only)